SHW

ALLEN COUNTY PUBLIC LIBRARY

658.1592 F91

Friendly Quicken for windows

Quicken for Windows™

The LeBlond Group

BANTAM BOOKS

NEW YORK • TORONTO • LONDON • SYDNEY • AUCKLAND

Allen County Public Library
900 Webster Street
PO Box 2270
Fort Wayne, IN 46801-2270

Friendly Quicken for Windows™
A Bantam Book / February 1993

All rights reserved.
Copyright © 1993 by The LeBlond Group
Cover design © 1993 by Bantam Books
Interior design by Nancy Sugihara
Produced by Micro Text Productions, Inc.
Composed by Context Publishing Services

This book may not be reproduced in whole
or in part, by mimeograph or any other means,
without permission.
For information address: Bantam Books

Throughout the book, tradenames and trademarks of
some companies and products have been used, and no
such uses are intended to convey endorsement of or
other affiliations with the book.

ISBN 0-553-56216-9

Published simultaneously in the United States and Canada

Bantam Books are published by Bantam Books, a division of
Bantam Doubleday Dell Publishing Group, Inc. Its trademark,
consisting of the words "Bantam Books" and the portrayal of
a rooster, is Registered in U.S. Patent and Trademark Office
and in other countries. Marca Registrada, Bantam Books,
666 Fifth Avenue, New York, New York 10103.

PRINTED IN CANADA

0   9   8   7   6   5   4   3   2   1

Contents

13 The Reconciliation Process: Working in the Reconcile Window   79

14 The Reconciliation Process: Completing the Reconciliation   89

15 The Reconciliation Process: Printing Reconciliation Reports   93

16 Writing Checks   99

17 Printing Checks   103

Preface

Most of us become computer users because we have to, because knowledge of a particular software package is needed for a job, or because computer-assisted productivity is essential to success in business. There are hundreds of reasons. Computers and software are only the means to an end. They have become a necessity of life, and this requirement shapes the way we go about learning how to use software.

Not everyone is interested in every detail of a particular program. Here is a quick, no-nonsense introduction that teaches the basic skills needed to use the software.

In approximately 200 pages, each Friendly Computer Book covers the basic features of a specific popular software in a way that will get new users up and running quickly. The result is a series of computer books that has these unifying characteristics:

- **Topic-oriented organization.** Short, self-contained lessons focus on a particular topic or area that is important in learning to use the software.

When you finish the lesson, you'll have mastered an aspect of the software.

- **Spacious layout.** Large type and a spacious layout make the books easy on the eyes and easy to use.
- **Step-by-step approach.** Numbered lists help you to concentrate on the practical steps needed to get your work done.
- **Numerous screen shots.** Each lesson contains at least two screen shots that show you exactly how your screen should look.
- **Frequent use of icons.** Many eye-catching icons—drawing attention to important aspects of the text and software—are placed throughout the book.
- **Lay-flat binding.** Friendly Computer Books stay open as you work.
- **And finally, a low, low price.**

For many users Friendly Computer Books are all they'll need. For others who want to learn more about the software, we've suggested further readings.

Enjoy the friendly approach of Friendly Computer Books!

Ron Petrusha
Series Editor

1

Getting Started

Why Quicken?

Is following a household budget a nightmare? Does keeping your checkbook balanced send you into a tizzy? Quicken for Windows is just the software you'll need to get your financial household in order. Designed for home or small business use, this program will take the hassle out of balancing your budget.

Installing Quicken for Windows

When you run the Quicken for Windows Install program, it copies all the appropriate files to your hard disk and creates a group window in Program Manager. Along the way, it asks you about your installation preferences and later lets you modify them, should you change your mind.

To install Quicken for Windows on your PC, you must have approximately 1.5 megabytes of free disk space available, plus an additional 1.5 megabytes if you wish to install the Quicken Tutorial.

Here are the steps to install the software:

1. Place Install Disk 1 in drive B. (Of course, if you're using the 5.25 inch disks, insert the disk in drive A and substitute that drive letter in the steps that follow.)
2. With Windows Program Manager active, click on **File** in the Menu bar and then **Run** from the pull-down menu that appears. Figure 1.1 shows the dialog box that you'll see at this stage.
3. Type **b:install** and then click on **OK**. You'll see the dialog box shown in Figure 1.2 listing Quicken's default installation settings. These settings specify:

   - The floppy drive containing the Install Disk.
   - The subdirectory C:\QUICKENW in which the Quicken files (and your Quicken data files) will be placed.
   - In Windows, that the Quicken icon is placed in a group window of its own.
   - That Billminder runs whenever you open Windows. (Billminder uses your PC's system clock and acts as a reminder whenever post-dated checks need to be mailed.)

4. If you want to change one of these installation settings, simply click on its button to open a dialog box. For example, if you click on the **To**

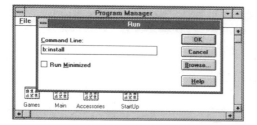

Figure 1.1 The Run dialog box

button in Figure 1.2, you'll access a dialog box where you can change which subdirectory the Quicken files will be placed in. When you click on **OK**, you'll be returned to the dialog box in Figure 1.2 where you can continue to make changes to the installation settings.

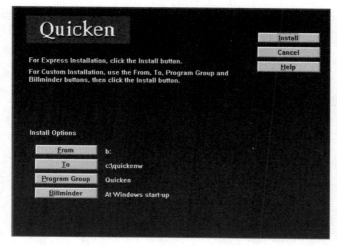

Figure 1.2 Quicken Install settings

Figure 1.3   When installation
is complete

5. Click on **Install** to begin the installation process.
    After Install has copied all the Quicken program
    and sample files to disk, you'll see the message in
    Figure 1.3. (If you're using 5 1/4 inch disks, you'll
    be prompted to insert Install Disk 2 in the drive.)
6. Click on **OK** to return to Program Manager. Your
    screen should look similar to Figure 1.4 with a
    new Quicken group window and associated
    icons.

Figure 1.4   The new Quicken
group window

Starting Quicken

Once Quicken is installed on your system, you can double-click on its icon——in Program Manager to launch it. Before starting Quicken for the first time, though, read the next lesson and gather the financial information discussed there so that you can respond to Quicken's inquiries.

Exiting Quicken

To leave Quicken for Windows and return to the Program Manager, do one of the following:

- Choose **Exit** from the **File** menu.
- Press **Alt+F4**.
- Double-click on the window control box .

Don't worry about saving your files before leaving Quicken. Your work is saved for you automatically whenever you do anything in Quicken.

◆ *Lesson* ◆

2

Your First Quicken Session

Gathering Information to Start

Before you can begin to use Quicken for Windows, you'll need to gather some financial information so you can start your automated financial system at a particular point in time. The amount of financial information you'll need, however, depends on which Quicken features you immediately want to take advantage of.

Selecting a Starting Date

The first thing you must do is decide on a *starting date*, which represents the beginning date from which you'll enter and track transactions. The most natural starting date is January 1. That way, you'll record all income and expense data for the entire year in one place and enjoy the full benefits of Quicken's report-generating capability, especially for tax purposes. Another good alternative is to use the first day of a month. Remember though, if you choose this option, you'll then have

·
7

two financial systems for that year—the manual re-cord-keeping system you previously used, and Quicken for the remainder of the year.

Financial Information You'll Need

Quicken for Windows can play either a small role in your financial recordkeeping or act as your total financial system. The amount of financial information you'll need to start depends on:

- What information you want Quicken to track
- The starting date from which to begin tracking information

If, for example, you want to start using Quicken to monitor and balance your checkbook, you'll need only the beginning balance of your checking account on a specific starting date. If you want to track other accounts, such as savings and money market accounts, you'll also want to establish these balances on the same date.

Tip
There are two places to find your beginning balance for a checking account. For a particular starting date, you might want to use the corresponding balance from your paper check register. Another alternative is to use the beginning balance from a monthly bank statement—but make sure that you first add any open (outstanding) deposits and subtract any open checks and withdrawals.

If, however, you want to be able to create reports summarizing income and expenses by category, you really should enter financial information—such as checking account information—for the full year. Otherwise, reports you create at tax time won't reflect the full year.

Choosing Quicken Features

If you're new to Quicken, here's a word of advice: *Start slow*. Otherwise, you're likely to get bogged down in the breadth of features Quicken for Windows provides.

It's best to get one portion of your financial record-keeping running smoothly in Quicken, such as your checking account, before adding your savings and money market accounts. Once you're successfully using Quicken to balance your accounts, write and print checks, and act as a Billminder, then explore other areas such as generating budget comparisons and tax information, paying bills electronically, tracking investments, or calculating your net worth.

Running the Tutorial and Introduction to Quicken

The first time you start Quicken for Windows, you'll be asked whether you want to run the Tutorial or to see an Introduction to Quicken. The Tutorial teaches basic mouse and Windows skills you'll need to effectively use Quicken. The Introduction to Quicken provides a brief sketch of what Quicken for Windows offers. You can also run either at a later time through the Help Tutorials command.

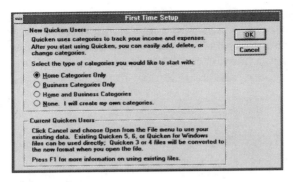

Figure 2.1 The First Time Setup dialog box

Specifying Starting Information

Quicken needs some minimal financial information from you to get started. After you decline to view (or go through) the tutorial and introduction to Quicken, you'll see the First Time Setup dialog box shown in Figure 2.1. (You won't see this dialog box the next time you open Quicken.)

Tip
If you've previously used a DOS version of Quicken, click on Cancel to bypass this dialog box and open Quicken for Windows. Then choose the File Open command and select your existing Quicken for DOS QDATA file.

Home and Business Categories

By default, Home Categories Only is chosen (checked). This tells Quicken the income and expense catego-

3 1833 02459 2484

ries—such as mortgage expense or salary expense—
you're most likely to need. If you plan to use Quicken
for home and business finances, click on the Home
and Business Categories radio button.

Setting up the Basic Checking Account

After you accept or change the First Time Setup settings, you'll see the Select Account Type dialog box
shown in Figure 2.2. Here Quicken asks you which
account you want to begin with. As you'll learn in
Lesson 3, you record transactions, such as checks and
deposits, in a specific account.

Quicken requests this account information so that
you can immediately start entering financial information. Try entering the account information shown in
Figures 2.2 and 2.3, or enter your own checking account information. Here are the steps:

1. Quicken makes the assumption that you'll be
   setting up a bank account, and sets the Account
   Type accordingly. Although you can change this
   setting by choosing another type, such as Credit
   Card, in most cases you won't want to do so.
   Instead, click on **OK** to access the New Account
   Information dialog box, where you can enter information about this bank account.
2. In the Account Name text box, add an account
   name by typing a descriptive name no longer
   than 15 characters, such as **Checking** in Figure
   2.3. Then press **Tab** or click on the **Balance** text
   box.

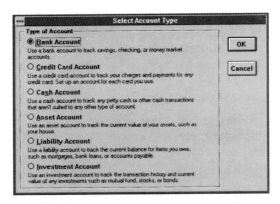

Figure 2.2 Specifying the type of account

3. In the Balance text box, enter the beginning balance of this Checking account—*don't* include a dollar sign; commas are optional. So, for the example in Figure 2.3, you can enter **5000**, **5,000**, or **5000.00**. When you press **Tab** or click on the **date** text box, Quicken changes this value to 5,000.00.

4. Either accept or change the date of this beginning balance. Quicken automatically provides today's

Figure 2.3 Entering new account information

date from your PC's system clock. To change this date to 8/1/92 as in Figure 2.3, type **8/1/92** in the same format Quicken uses.

Tip

In the date text box, pressing + increases the date displayed by one day; pressing – decreases the date by one day.

5. To enter an optional description, press **Tab** or click within the **Description** text box. You can then type a description up to 21 characters. In Figure 2.3, for example, typing **Coast Savings 116394** identifies the bank and account number of this checking account.

6. When all the information is complete, click on **OK**.

Now Quicken for Windows has all the information it needs to get started. The program uses the account information you just supplied and opens a register window like the one in Figure 2.4 named Checking, which contains the $5,000 Opening Balance on 8/1/92. Entering transactions in this register is discussed in Lesson 4. But first, Lesson 3 explains account, register, and transaction basics.

Location of Quicken Data Files

When you install Quicken for Windows, a new directory—C:\QUICKENW—is created to hold the Quicken

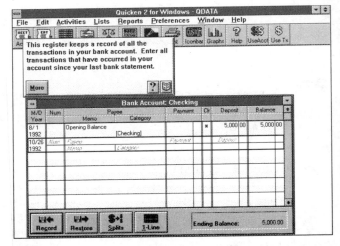

Figure 2.4 The Quicken check register with setup account data

program files (unless you specified otherwise during installation, of course). This directory also acts as a repository for your data file, which Quicken names QDATA.

◆ *Lesson* ◆

3

Account, Register, and Transaction Basics

What is an Account?

In Quicken, an account is what you would expect—related transactions for which you keep a balance. For example, the basic checking account suggested by Quicken is, in general, composed of income (deposits) and expenses (checks). A running balance is maintained and adjusted after each transaction, just as you do in a paper check register.

Each of your paper accounts can be represented by a corresponding account in Quicken. If you have two checking accounts, a savings account, and a money market account, you would create four accounts in Quicken to track each one individually. (Creating new accounts is discussed in Lesson 25.)

As you become comfortable with Quicken, you may also create other accounts to track transactions. For example, you can create a liability account to keep track of a mortgage, an investment account to mirror your stock and bond portfolio at a brokerage firm, or a credit card account to track a specific credit card balance determined by charges, interest, and payments.

Regardless of what type of account you're working with, each is composed of transactions, which are recorded in a register.

What is a Register?

Once you create an account, such as the checking account opened in Lesson 2, the *register* acts just like a paper check register; it holds all the information for a particular account. It is where expenses (checks) and income (deposits) are recorded and a running balance is maintained. Once you've entered information in a register, you can then take advantage of Quicken features such as reconciling the account against your bank statement, allocating expenses to categories, and generating financial reports.

Each account has its own separate register. Figure 3.1 shows the Checking register Quicken opened for the account you created in Lesson 2 with a check and deposit entered. (You'll learn how to enter these transactions in Lesson 4.)

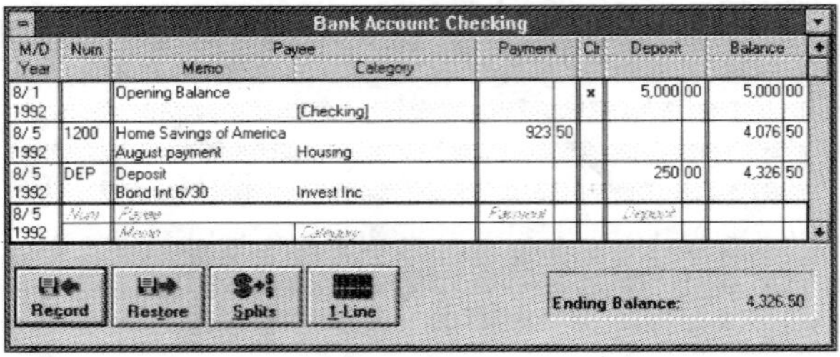

M/D Year	Num	Payee / Memo / Category	Payment	Clr	Deposit	Balance	
8/1 1992		Opening Balance / [Checking]		x	5,000 00	5,000 00	
8/5 1992	1200	Home Savings of America / August payment / Housing	923 50			4,076 50	
8/5 1992	DEP	Deposit / Bond Int 6/30 / Invest Inc			250 00	4,326 50	
8/5 1992	*Num*	*Payee* / *Memo* / *Category*	*Payment*		*Deposit*		

Record   Restore   Splits   1-Line   **Ending Balance:**   4,326.50

Figure 3.1 A register for a new account

What is a Transaction?

The register is used to enter each *transaction* that corresponds to a particular account. In Figure 3.1, for example, a transaction is any of the following:

- Income, such as a paycheck deposit, interest earned on the monthly balance, or the $250 bond interest income.
- An expense, such as check 1200 shown in the figure, a monthly service charge, an ATM cash withdrawal, or an automatic payment
- A transfer between accounts, such as from savings to checking

Notice that each transaction is composed of two lines, one white and one yellow (or gray if you don't have a color monitor). These lines are made up of *fields*—text boxes where you enter information. At a minimum, each transaction must include a date, a description, and an amount. For example, because check 1200 is an expense, it is composed of at least the Date, Num, Payee, and Payment fields in Figure 3.1.

At a minimum, a deposit is composed of the Date, Payee, and Deposit fields. Notice that these fields were used to create the $250 deposit in Figure 3.1.

Tip

As you'll see in Lesson 4, using text in the Num field of a deposit can help you generate reports and search for transactions.

The C (Cleared) field is used when you're reconciling the account to indicate that a transaction—such as a check—has cleared. (You'll see how to do this in Lesson 13.)

In both cases, the Memo and Category fields are optional. The Memo field allows you to include a descriptive phrase about the particular transaction; for example, check 1200 in Figure 3.1 includes the memo "August payment." The Category field allows you to allocate a transaction to an expense or income category; for instance, the $250 bond interest is allocated to the Inv Inc (investment income) category. (Assigning categories is covered in Lesson 5.

When you've finished entering a transaction, Quicken automatically calculates the current balance and enters it in the Balance field. *You don't enter this amount, nor can you change it.* In Figure 3.1, for instance, Quicken subtracts the 923.50 amount of check 1200 from the 5,000.00 Opening Balance and enters the 4,076.50 result in check 1200's Balance field. Likewise, Quicken adds the 250.00 deposit to the prior balance and enters the new balance of 4,326.50 in the 8/5 deposit Balance field.

◆ *Lesson* ◆

4

Entering Transactions

Entering a Check

Starting with the Checking register window Quicken opened for you in Lesson 2, let's enter check 1200 shown in Figure 4.1—or better yet, enter a check of your own instead.

 Tip

When you write a Quicken check, the transaction is automatically entered in the register for you. See Lesson 16.

1. When a register is first opened, the cursor resides at the beginning of the first blank transaction. Two thick black lines outline the fields of this transaction; all fields are white indicating that it is the active transaction. If you've been experimenting with Quicken and a blank transaction isn't selected, choose the **Edit New Transaction** command, or press its shortcut, **Ctrl+N**.

		Bank Account: Checking					
M/D Year	Num	Payee	Payment	Clr	Deposit	Balance	
		Memo Category					
8/1 1992		Opening Balance [Checking]		x	5,000 00	5,000 00	
8/5 1992	1200	*Payee*	*Payment*		*Deposit*		
	ATM Deposit EFT Next Chk# Print	*Category*					

Record | Restore | Splits | 1-Line | | Ending Balance: | 5,000.00

Figure 4.1 Entering a check

2. In the Date field, either accept the current date that Quicken provides or enter a new one in the same date format. To enter the date exactly as you see it in Figure 4.1 keep pressing **Del** to erase the existing date, and then type **8/5/92**. When you press **Tab** or click on the **Num** field, Quicken changes this date entry to read 8/5 on the first line and 1992 on the second line of the Date field.

Tip

Press **t** in the Date field to paste the current date; **m** for the first day of the current month and **h** for the last day; **y** for the first day of the current year and **r** for the last day. And remember that you can press + and – to change the date by one day.

3. In the Num field, enter the check number, **1200** in the current example. (You'll see how to use the drop-down list that appears in the next example.) Press **Tab** to move to the Payee field.

Tip

After you enter the first check in a register, pressing + in the Num field enters a check number one greater than the last one entered in the register; pressing – twice creates a check number two less than the last check entered.

4. In the Payee field, type the payee's name, **Home Mortgage of America** for this example. The name may be up to 37 characters long. Press **Tab** to move to the Payment field.

Tip

If the Payee field is too narrow to display all the text, expand the size of the window.

5. In the Payment field, type the amount of the check without a dollar sign. For the current example, type **923.50**. You can enter a number as large as 9,999,999.99.

Tip

Press Shift+Tab to move back to the previous field.

6. If you want to add the memo shown in Figure 4.2, press **Tab** to move to the Memo field and then type **August payment**.

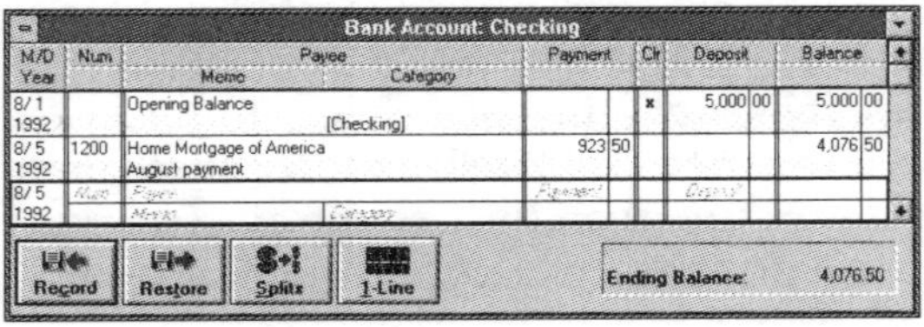

Figure 4.2   The register after entering check 1200

7. To confirm this transaction, click on **Record** at the bottom of the register. (To cancel a transaction before saving it, click on Restore.)

Quicken beeps as it records the check as a permanent transaction, and then adds a new blank transaction at the bottom of the register as shown in Figure 4.2. The cursor moves to the Date field in this new transaction.

You can see in Figure 4.2 how Quicken calculates a new account balance of $4,076.50 in check 1200's Balance field. The total Ending Balance for the entire Checking account also appears in the bottom right corner of the register.

Entering a Deposit

Entering a deposit works much like entering a check. Try entering the $250 deposit made on 8/5 shown in Figure 4.3, or one of your own, using these steps:

1. Make sure that the cursor resides in the Date field of a new blank transaction. If you've been experimenting with Quicken and a blank transaction isn't selected, press **Ctrl+N**, the shortcut for the Edit New Transaction command.

M/D Year	Num	Payee		Payment	Ck	Deposit	Balance	
		Memo	Category					
8/5 1992	1200	Home Mortgage of America August payment		923 50			4,076 50	
8/5 1992	DEP	Deposit Home Mortgage of America		*Payment*		*Deposit*		

Bank Account: Checking

Record **Restore** **Splits** **1-Line** **Ending Balance:** 4,076.50

Figure 4.3 Entering a deposit

2. In the Date field, either accept the current date Quicken automatically provides or enter another one in the same date format. (Don't forget about using + and – to change the displayed date.) In Figure 4.3, for example, Quicken automatically uses the date from the previous transaction, 8/5 1992, which is fine in this case. Press **Tab** or click on the **Num** field.

3. In the Num field, type **D** or click on **DEP** in the drop-down list that appears. Then press **Tab** or click on the **Payee** field.

Tip
Although adding text in the Num field is optional, text such as DEP makes it easier to search for similar transactions and to create filtered reports.

4. In the Payee field, enter a description of 37 characters or fewer; for example, **Deposit** as shown in Figure 4.3. Press **Tab** to move to the Deposit field.

Tip

Quicken only memorizes transactions that include an entry in the Payee field.

---

5. In the Deposit field, type the amount of the deposit without a dollar sign. In the current example, type either **250.00** or **250**. You can enter a number as large as 9,999,999.99. If a deposit represents a transaction *between* accounts, such as a transfer from a savings account, see Lesson 26.

6. If you want to add the memo shown in Figure 4.4, press **Tab** to move to the Memo field, and then type **Bond Int 6/30**.

7. Click on **Record** to confirm this transaction.

Quicken beeps as it records this deposit as a permanent transaction and then adds a new blank transaction at the bottom of the register. The cursor moves to the Date field in this new transaction. Quicken also calculates a new checking account balance of $4,326.50 in the Balance field.

Tip

The Payee drop-down list includes all transactions to date that Quicken has memorized. In Figure 4.3, for instance, notice how the description of the check just entered, "Home Mortgage of America," appears. By clicking on a description in this list (or typing letters until Quicken finishes the description you want), you can easily re-create recurring transactions, such as a mortgage payment. For example, if you click on "Home Mortgage of America," Quicken would add this to the Payee field. Each time you press Tab (don't click) to move to a different field in the transaction, what you previously entered is filled in. For instance, in the Payment field Quicken would enter 923.50 for you, the amount in Figure 4.2. You'll learn more about memorized transactions in Lesson 19.

Entering Other Withdrawals

Other withdrawals—automated teller machine withdrawals, service charges, wire transfers, and automatic payments—are entered in virtually the same way as a check except that a check number isn't included. For instance, try entering the $200 cash withdrawal in Figure 4.4 made at an automated teller on 8/3/92.

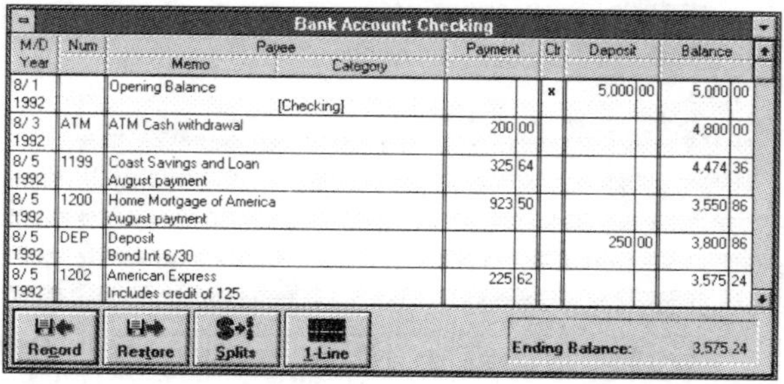

M/D Year	Num	Payee / Memo / Category	Payment		Clr	Deposit	Balance	
8/1 1992		Opening Balance [Checking]			x	5,000 00	5,000 00	
8/3 1992	ATM	ATM Cash withdrawal	200 00				4,800 00	
8/5 1992	1199	Coast Savings and Loan August payment	325 64				4,474 36	
8/5 1992	1200	Home Mortgage of America August payment	923 50				3,550 86	
8/5 1992	DEP	Deposit Bond Int 6/30				250 00	3,800 86	
8/5 1992	1202	American Express Includes credit of 125	225 62				3,575 24	

Bank Account: Checking

Record Restore Splits 1-Line   Ending Balance: 3,575.24

Figure 4.4 How Quicken sorts transactions

How Quicken Sorts Transactions

When you enter transactions in a register, Quicken sorts the transactions by date. For instance, when you click on Record to confirm the 8/3/92 ATM cash withdrawal in Figure 4.4, Quicken places the ATM withdrawal before check 1200 even though it was entered after this check.

Quicken further sorts transactions that occur on the same date by check number. To see how this works, try entering checks 1199 and check 1202 shown in Figure 4.4. Although both were written on 8/5/92, Quicken sorts the register so that check 1199 appears first, then check 1200, and finally check 1202. Notice, also, that check 1202 appears after the 8/5 deposit because, of the two, the deposit was entered first.

Entering Postdated Transactions

A *postdated transaction* is dated in the future, such as check 1201 in Figure 4.5 written on 8/5/92 but dated 8/15/92. Typically, a postdated check won't be hon-

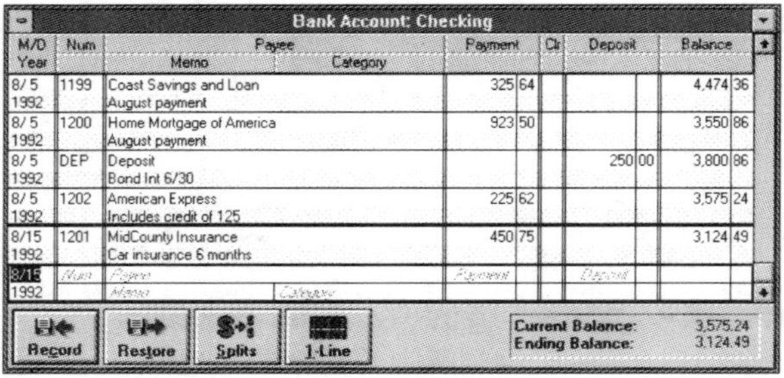

M/D Year	Num	Payee / Memo Category	Payment	Cl	Deposit	Balance
8/5 1992	1199	Coast Savings and Loan / August payment	325 64			4,474 36
8/5 1992	1200	Home Mortgage of America / August payment	923 50			3,550 86
8/5 1992	DEP	Deposit / Bond Int 6/30			250 00	3,800 86
8/5 1992	1202	American Express / Includes credit of 125	225 62			3,575 24
8/15 1992	1201	MidCounty Insurance / Car insurance 6 months	450 75			3,124 49
8/15 1992	*Num*	*Payee* / *Memo* *Category*	*Payment*		*Deposit*	

Bank Account: Checking

Record   Restore   Splits   1-Line

Current Balance: 3,575.24
Ending Balance: 3,124.49

Figure 4.5   Entering a postdated check

ored by a bank until the date on the check. That's why Quicken uses a thick blue line to separate current and postdated transaction and then calculates two account balances for a register. The Current Balance of $3,575.24 reflects all transactions up to and including today's date (which Quicken gets from your PC's system clock). The Ending Balance of $3,124.49 also incorporates the postdated transaction. Of course, only the Ending Balance of $3,575.24 will appear when you open this register on or after 8/15/92.

Tip
By postdating checks, you can use Billminder to remind you when checks should be paid. See Lesson 21.

5

Assigning a Transaction to a Category

What is a Category?

Quicken provides a number of categories shown in the Category & Transfer List window in Figure 5.1. Assigning a *category* to a transaction allows you to group related income and expenses. By assigning each check you write for medical expense to the Medical category, for example, you can keep track of year-to-date medical expenses. This categorization then makes it possible to easily track income and deductions for income tax purposes.

Managing the Category List is important if you're using categories for tax purposes. See Lesson 22.

Try opening the Category & Transfer List window by clicking on in the IconBar or pressing Ctrl+C, both shortcuts for the Lists Category & Transfer command. Quicken opens the window shown in Figure 5.1 and makes it the active window. To close this window,

Figure 5.1 The Category List

double-click on its window control box  or press Ctrl+F4.

The Category List is organized alphabetically, first by income categories followed by expense categories. A subcategory (Sub) is a subset of a category. Loan, for example, is a subcategory of Auto. (See Lesson 23.)

Adding a Category to a Transaction

Categories may be assigned to a new transaction or added later. Assuming you've been following along and created the register that now appears in Figure 5.1, the following are the steps necessary to assign a category to check 1199. You can also follow these steps to assign a category to your own transactions:

1. Move to the Category field of the transaction to which you want to add a category. In Figure 5.2, simply click on check 1199's **Category** field.

2. In the Category drop-down list that appears, scroll down and double-click on your choice. (If you need to, click on  to open this list.) In this

			Bank Account: Checking				
M/D Year	Num	Payee / Memo / Category		Payment	Cl	Deposit	Balance
8/5 1992	1199	Coast Savings and Loan August payment · Auto:Loan		325 64			4,474 36
8/5 1992	1200	Home Mortgage of America · Auto August payment · Auto:Fuel		923 50			3,550 86
8/5 1992	DEP	Deposit · Auto:Loan Bond Int 6/30 · Auto:Service Bank Chrg				250 00	3,800 86
8/5 1992	1202	American Express Includes credit of 125		225 62			3,575 24
8/15 1992	1201	MidCounty Insurance Car insurance 6 months		450 75			3,124 49
8/10 1992							

Record	Restore	Splits	1-Line	Current Balance:	3,575.24
				Ending Balance:	3,124.49

Figure 5.2   Assigning a category

example, double-click on the **Auto:Loan** subcategory.

Tip

The Category drop-down list allows you to assign a category without opening the Category &
Transfer List window. It is categorized alphabetically, however, rather than by income and expense.

3. Add the category to check 1199 by clicking on
Record at the bottom of the register window.

Tip

Quicken has an auto-completion feature that
can help you enter a category. If you type **T** in
the Category field, Quicken fills in "Taxes," the
first category beginning with T; type **Te**, and
the entry changes to "Telephone," the first category beginning with Te. To enter a subcategory
such as Auto Loan, type **Auto:** and Quicken

adds the first Auto subcategory, Fuel. You can now use the + and – keys to scroll through the subcategories. Press +, for instance, and Quicken replaces "Fuel" with "Loan", the second Auto subcategory.

Figure 5.3 shows other categories assigned to each of the transactions in the Checking register window. If you've been following along with the example, try entering them yourself, as you'll see these categories used in following lessons.

Tip

You can assign multiple categories to a transaction, which is known as *splitting a transaction*. For instance, you could assign an ATM withdrawal to three categories: groceries, auto fuel, and miscellaneous. You'll see how to do this in Lesson 24.

		Bank Account: Checking					
M/D Year	Num	Payee / Memo / Category	Payment	Clr	Deposit	Balance	
8/ 3 1992	ATM	ATM Cash withdrawal / Misc	200 00			4,800 00	
8/ 5 1992	1199	Coast Savings and Loan / August payment / Auto:Loan	325 64			4,474 36	
8/ 5 1992	1200	Home Mortgage of America / August payment / Housing	923 50			3,550 86	
8/ 5 1992	DEP	Deposit / Bond Int 6/30 / Invest Inc			250 00	3,800 86	
8/ 5 1992	1202	American Express / Includes credit of 125 / Entertain	225 62			3,575 24	
8/15 1992	1201	MidCounty Insurance / Car insurance 6 months / Insurance	450 75			3,124 49	

Record	Restore	Splits	1-Line		Current Balance: 3,575.24 Ending Balance: 3,124.49

Figure 5.3   Assigning categories to all transactions

6

Working with Quicken's Windows

What is a Window?

Before proceeding any further, it's important to ensure that everyone understands how Quicken uses windows to present information. In Quicken, a *window* represents a location where related information is stored, or where you enter related information. We've already worked with both situations; a register window, in which we entered transactions from one account; and a Category & Transfer List window, which represents a list of categories you can assign.

In Quicken, you can have multiple windows open at once, allowing you to easily work on related tasks. You can, for example, jump back and forth between a Checking register window and the Reconcile window when balancing your checking account (described in Lesson 13).

Quicken offers these basic window types:

- Registers for accounts—for example, a checking account or credit card account register

- Lists—for example, the Category & Transfer List or the Account List
- Task-related windows—for example, the Reconcile window and Pay Credit Card Bill window
- Command-related windows—for example, the Edit Find window (you'll see these in only a few cases)
- Reports—for example, a cash flow report

The Components of a Window

Figure 6.1 shows the components of a Quicken window, and below is a description of each component:

Window control box Clicking once on this box opens the window control menu, which allows you to size, position, or close the window using the keyboard.

Window control box   Title bar   Scroll bar

Window control menu   Minimize button

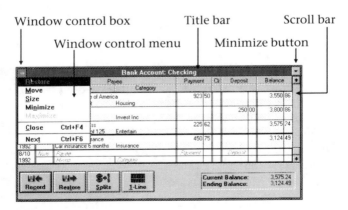

Figure 6.1   The components of a window

Title bar
This portion of the window contains the window's title. The window in Figure 6.1, for instance, contains the Checking account register.

Minimize button ▣
Clicking on this box shrinks the window to an icon in the Quicken window.

Scroll bar
Lets you scroll the window's contents up or down.

The Active Window

In order to do anything in a window, such as enter transactions in the Checking register window in Figure 6.1, it must be *active*. The active window is the one whose title bar is highlighted.

When more than one window is open in Quicken, you can activate a specific window using any of the following techniques:

- Click on its **title bar**
- Select the **Window** command and choose the window from the pull-down menu
- Press **Ctrl+F6** to cycle (move) between open windows until the window you want is active

Moving a Window

The easiest way to move a window is by clicking on its title bar. Then, keeping the mouse depressed, drag the window to a new location.

Resizing a Window

By far, the easiest way to resize a window is to use the mouse. To decrease the size of the Checking register window in Figure 6.1 as an exercise, follow these steps:

1. Move the mouse to the lower right-hand corner of the window until it turns into a double-sided arrow.
2. Keeping the mouse button depressed, drag the corner inward. In Figure 6.2, for instance, the lower right-hand corner of the register is being dragged inward.
3. When you reach the size you want, release the mouse button. The size of the window should now resemble Figure 6.3.

To change the width of the window, position the mouse along the left or right side of the window; to change the height, position the mouse along the top or bottom side.

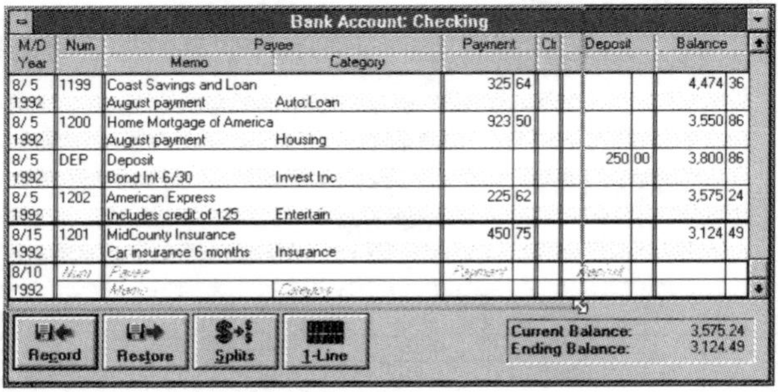

Figure 6.2 Resizing a window

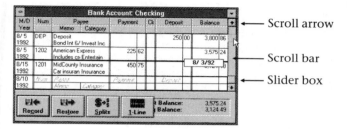

Figure 6.3 Scrolling with the mouse

⇨ **Note:** Quicken won't let you decrease some windows, such as a register window, below a certain size.

Scrolling within a Window

To scroll through the contents of a window, use the scroll bar shown in Figure 6.3. Try clicking on the top arrow ▣ and you'll see that the cursor moves up one item—one transaction in this register window; clicking on ▣ moves the cursor down one transaction. Clicking the scroll bar above the slider box moves up one windowful; clicking below the slider box moves down one windowful.

Dragging the slider box upward moves the cursor to earlier transactions; dragging downward moves to later transactions. If you moved the slider box to the very top of the scroll bar in Figure 6.3, you'd end up at the first transaction in the register, the opening balance on 8/1/92.

Tip

As you drag the slider box in a Register window, Quicken displays the date of the transaction that will appear at the top of the window when you release the mouse button. In Figure 6.3, for instance, the date 8/3/92 appears, which corresponds to the only transaction on that date, an ATM withdrawal of $200.00.

Table 6.1 defines how to use the keyboard to move around in a window.

Tip

You can collapse transactions to a single line by clicking on the ▦ icon.

Minimizing a Window

To minimize a window, click on the Minimize button ▾ in the upper right-hand corner of the window. This reduces a window to an icon within the Quicken window. For example, clicking on ▾ in Figure 6.3 reduces the Check register window to 🏛. To restore a window to its previous size, double-click on its icon.

Closing a Window

The two easiest ways to close an open, active window are:

- Double-clicking on its window control box ▭.
- Pressing Ctrl+F4.

Table 6.1   Moving with the Keyboard

Key	Moves
↑ or ↓	Up or down to the next item.
PgUp or PgDn	Up or down a windowful
Ctrl+Home	To the first item in a window
Ctrl+End	To the last item in a window
Ctrl+PgUp	To the first transaction in the current month and then to the first transaction in the previous month
Ctrl+PgDn	To the first transaction in the next month
Home+Home	To the first field in a transaction
Home+Home +Home	To the first transaction in a window
Home+Home +Home+Home	To the first transaction in a register
End+End	To the last field in a transaction
End+End+End	To the last transaction in a window
End+End +End+End	To the last transaction in a register

If you're closing a Register window and a new transaction has not yet been saved, Quicken will display a message box alerting you. Click on Yes if you want to save the transaction before closing.

To close all open windows, use the Window Close All Windows command.

7

Moving Around in Quicken

Opening a Pull-Down Menu

Like other Windows applications, the *menu bar* near the top of the Quicken window contains commands that access pull-down menus. To activate a pull-down menu, such as the File menu in Figure 7.1, click on the command in the menu bar; to close a pull-down menu, press Esc or click elsewhere in Quicken outside of the menu.

The unique features of a pull-down menu, as shown in Figure 7.1, are:

- The ... (ellipses) immediately following a menu item, such as Print Checks, which indicate that the item leads to a dialog box.
- The ▶ (arrow) to the right of an item, such as the one after Passwords, means that it leads to a *cascade* menu. A cascade menu is a submenu attached to the right side of a menu item.
- *Shortcut keys* to the right of a menu item name means you can bypass the pull-down menu by

Figure 7.1 The File menu

pressing that key combination. For example, pressing Ctrl+P is a shortcut for the File Print Register command.

- A *grayed option* (not shown) means that choice is not currently available.

To select a pulldown-menu item, such as Print Register on the File menu, use one of these techniques:

- Click on the item, **Print Register**.
- Press ↓ to highlight Print Register and then press **Enter**.
- Press **p**, the item's *pneumonic* or underlined letter.

The dialog box shown in Figure 7.2 then appears.

Using Icons as Shortcuts

The IconBar at the top of the Quicken window provides shortcuts for many commonly used Quicken commands. For example, clicking on the Print icon 🖨 accesses the Print Register dialog box shown in Figure 7.2.

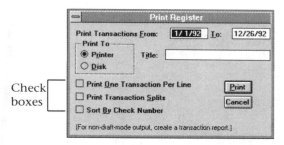

Check boxes

Figure 7.2   The Print Register dialog box

Tip
The Preferences Iconbar command presents a dialog box in which you can select options to hide (and reveal) the IconBar icons and their text.

Elements of a Dialog Box

A number of Quicken commands access a dialog box, which then requests information from you. Figure 7.2, above, and Figure 7.3 are two typical examples. To see how to maneuver in a dialog box, try the following:

1. Open the Print Checks dialog box by clicking on **File** in the menu bar, and then on **Print Checks** in the file pull-down menu. The cursor resides in the First Check Number text box where the initial text 1001 is highlighted. A *text box* accepts text input in the same way that a transaction field does in a Register window. (Lesson 9 explains how to move within and edit a text

Drop-down list

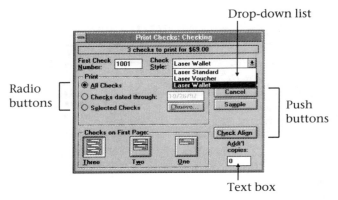

Radio buttons

Push buttons

Text box

Figure 7.3   The Print Checks dialog box

box.) Enter a different check number in this text box; for this exercise, type **2000**.

2. Move to the Check Style drop-down list by clicking on the portion of the list you can see—for example, **Laser Standard**. A *drop-down list* presents a fixed number of choices. For example, here you'll open the three-item list in Figure 7.3. Click on one of the choices—for example, **Laser Wallet**—to select it.

3. Make a selection from the Print options by clicking on one of the three *radio buttons*, which allow you to choose one item from a group of options. In this case, click on the **Checks dated through:** radio button to turn this option on. For now, let's accept the default date in the text box to the right.

4. Make a Checks on First Page selection by clicking on the **Two** button. (These options work just like radio buttons—you can choose only one.)

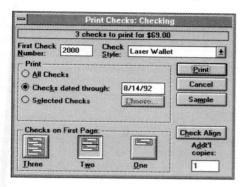

Figure 7.4 Specifying settings in the
Print Checks dialog box

5. Specify the number of extra copies by pressing
   Tab to move to the Addt'l copies text box. Then
   type **1**. (If you click on this text box instead
   of pressing Tab, press **Del** to erase the current
   entry before you begin typing.) The settings in
   this dialog box should now look like those in
   Figure 7.4.

 Tip
Tab and Shift+Tab move you to the next and
previous items.

6. Choose one of the four pushbuttons on the right
   of Figure 7.4 by clicking on it. A *pushbutton* initiates an action. For instance, the Print pushbutton
   initiates printing checks. In this case, click on
   Cancel (or press **Esc**) to close the dialog box yet
   retain your settings.

In some dialog boxes, such as the Print Register dialog box in Figure 7.2, you may also see check boxes. A *check box* acts like a switch—an X appears in the check box when it is turned on. Unlike radio buttons, check boxes are not mutually exclusive, so you can choose one, some, or all of the options. Click on a check box to turn it on or off.

◆ *Lesson* ◆

8

Using Quicken's Help

Using Quicken Qcards

Quicken 2.0 for Windows now includes Qcards, which are small windows containing directions that automatically appear whenever you use certain Quicken features. For example, Figure 8.1 shows the first Qcard that appears when you create a new account. Try clicking on the ? button in the lower-right corner of a Qcard window, and you'll branch to Quicken's help system where you'll see additional information about the feature or option at hand. Similarly, if you click on , you'll see a reference to a page number in the Quicken *User's Guide*.

> Choose the type of account you would like to create by clicking its button. Most people start with a bank account. Then click OK.
>
> ? 📖

Figure 8.1 Qcards provide on screen directions

Figure 8.2 Controlling when Qcards appear

By default Qcards appear all the time. By selecting the Preferences Qcards command, you can have Qcards appear in only certain circumstances or eliminate their appearance altogether.

Accessing Help

If you're having difficulty with a particular aspect of Quicken, try using Quicken's Help. Quicken uses the standard Windows Help system to offer a wealth of useful information organized by topic. To access Help:

- Press **F1** or choose the Help icon ❓ in the IconBar. Quicken starts the Windows Help system and displays information about the particular aspect of Quicken you happen to be working on; this is referred to as *context-sensitive* help.

- Click on **Help** in the menu bar. Then click on an item from the pull-down menu that appears. Here's a description of the three most important options:

  — Quicken Help—Provides context-sensitive help for the aspect of Quicken currently in use.

— How To Use Help—Explains how to use the Help system.

— Tutorials—Runs the Quicken or Windows Tutorial.

Navigating in Help

Try accessing Quicken's Help and navigating among Help topics by following these steps:

1. With a Checking register window active, select the **Help Index** command (or press F1). Quicken starts the Windows Help system, which displays the context-sensitive window shown in Figure 8.3. Additional Help topics are in green and appear underlined.

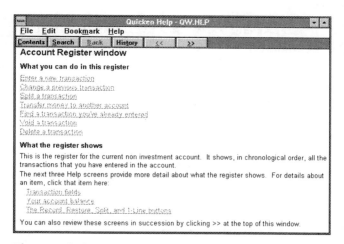

Figure 8.3 Quicken's context-sensitive Help

2. Select another topic—for example, **Delete a Transaction**—by moving the mouse pointer toward the topic until its shape changes to a hand with a pointing finger. Click once, and you'll move to another window that explains how to delete transactions.

3. At this point, you can click on one of the buttons at the top of the Help window to move within Help:

   - **Contents** displays the main index of Quicken Help topics.
   - **Search** allows you to search for a specific topic.
   - **Back** moves you to the previous Help screen.
   - **History** displays a list of Help topics you've already referenced, with the most recent topic first.
   - << and >>, when active, mean that there are Help topics grouped together through which you can browse using these buttons.

4. To quit the Windows Help system, either press **Alt+F4**, double-click on the Help window control box ▣ , or select Help's **File Exit** command.

Searching Help for a Specific Topic

You can also search for help on a specific topic. For example, suppose you want to get help for the topic "account lists." Try this approach:

1. Press **F1** or click on 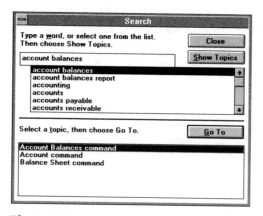 in the IconBar to start the Windows Help system.
2. Click on **Search** in the Help button bar to see an alphabetical list of topics like the one in Figure 8.4.
3. Specify the topic you're looking for by choosing a topic from the list or by typing a word or phrase you think is appropriate. For example, type **account** in the text box. Quicken moves to the first item in the list that includes "account"—in this case account balances—and enters it in the text box. (If account balances isn't the correct topic, you can scroll down the list and choose another topic.)
4. Click on **Show Topics** to see three Help topics related to account balances in the second list box.

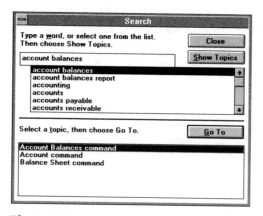

Figure 8.4 Searching Help for a topic

5. Go to a topic, such as **Account Balances command** by clicking on it and then clicking on **Go To**. Help takes you to information about the Reports Custom Account Balances command.

6. Quit the Windows Help system by double-clicking on the Help window control box ▣ .

Working with the Register

Selecting an Existing Transaction

After you've entered a transaction, such as a check or deposit, you may want to change a portion of it, delete it, or void it. To do so, you must first select the transaction. Suppose, for example, you want to change the transaction in Figure 9.1 representing check 1201 to MidCounty Insurance. (This register is the same as Figure 5.3.)

To select this transaction, simply click on any of its fields or use ↑ and ↓ until the cursor resides in the transaction. If you're going to edit a specific part of the transaction, such as the Description, click on that field.

Tip
To move to a transaction located a distance away, consider scrolling the register window (Lesson 6) or going to a specific transaction (Lesson 10).

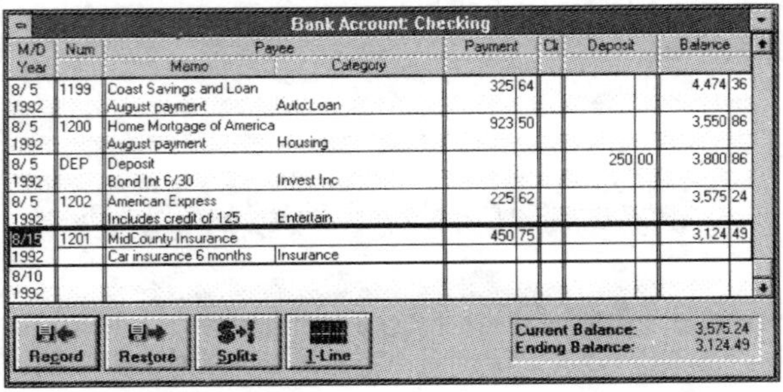

M/D Year	Num	Payee / Memo	Category	Payment		Ck	Deposit		Balance	
8/5 1992	1199	Coast Savings and Loan / August payment	Auto:Loan	325	64				4,474	36
8/5 1992	1200	Home Mortgage of America / August payment	Housing	923	50				3,550	86
8/5 1992	DEP	Deposit / Bond Int 6/30	Invest Inc				250	00	3,800	86
8/5 1992	1202	American Express / Includes credit of 125	Entertain	225	62				3,575	24
8/15 1992	1201	MidCounty Insurance / Car insurance 6 months	Insurance	450	75				3,124	49
8/10 1992										

Bank Account: Checking

Record / Restore / Splits / 1-Line

Current Balance: 3,575.24
Ending Balance: 3,124.49

Figure 9.1 Selecting the transaction for check 1201

Three things tell you that a transaction is selected:

- Thick black lines outline the transaction.
- Both lines of the transaction are the same color.
- The cursor resides in one of the fields.

Editing a Transaction

A field in a transaction is actually a text box, just like a text box in a dialog box. This means that the way you edit a transaction is very similar to editing data in a dialog box text box. Table 9.1 lists the keys you can use.

Referring back to Figure 9.1, for example, suppose you incorrectly entered the date of 8/15 and the $450.75 amount of check 1201. Instead, 8/5 and $350 are correct. Here's how to make these changes or to edit a transaction of your own:

1. Since the cursor resides in the Date field of the first blank transaction of Figure 9.1, click on the

check 1201 Date field. This selects the check 1201 transaction where 8/15 is selected and highlighted.

2. Change the date from 8/15 to 8/5 by pressing ← **twice** to move to the 1. Then press **Del** to delete this character.

Table 9.1   Keys That Edit Text in a Field

Key	Within a Field
Del	Deletes the character at the current location of the cursor or all highlighted characters.
Backspace	Deletes one character to the left.
Shift+→ or Shift+←	Shift+→ moves and selects (highlights) one character to the right. Shift+← moves and selects one character to the left. Keeping Shift depressed and pressing → or ← continues to select characters.
Home	Moves the cursor to the first character in the field.
→ or ←	Moves the cursor right or left one character.
End	Selects all characters in the field.
Ctrl+→ or Ctrl+←	Ctrl+→ moves to the beginning of the next word. Ctrl+← moves to the beginning of the previous word. Keeping Ctrl depressed and pressing → or Ctrl+← continues to move the cursor to the beginning of words.

3. Delete the existing amount by pressing **Tab** or clicking on the **Payment** field, where the entire amount will already be selected. Then press **Del** to erase this amount.

⇨ **Note:** If you select a field that includes a drop-down list—such as the Payee field—clicking on that field selects the current entry and opens the list. If you want, you can replace the entire entry by choosing an item in the list. Otherwise, press → or ← to unselect the text so you can make your edits.

4. Enter the new amount by typing **350.00** or **350**.

⚡ Unlike a word processing software package, Quicken doesn't allow you to use Ins to toggle between Insert and Typeover mode. Since Insert mode is always on, you must first delete text you want to replace.

5. Confirm these changes by clicking on **Record**. The cursor then moves to the Date field in the first blank transaction. Another alternative is to click on another transaction, or use ↑ or ↓ to move to another transaction. Then you'll see the message "Leaving Transaction. Record Changes?" Click on **Yes** to confirm and move to the transaction immediately above or below; click on No to cancel the changes and return to check 1201, the selected transaction; click on Cancel to accept the changes and return to the selected transaction.

M/D Year	Num	Payee / Memo / Category	Payment	Clr	Deposit	Balance	
8/ 5 1992	1199	Coast Savings and Loan August payment — Auto:Loan	325|64			4,474|36	
8/ 5 1992	1200	Home Mortgage of America August payment — Housing	923|50			3,550|86	
8/ 5 1992	DEP	Deposit Bond Int 6/30 — Invest Inc			250|00	3,800|86	
8/ 5 1992	1201	MidCounty Insurance Car insurance 6 months — Insurance	350|00			3,450|86	
8/ 5 1992	1202	American Express Includes credit of 125 — Entertain	225|62			3,225|24	
8/10 1992	Num	Payee Memo — Category	Payment		Deposit		

Bank Account: Checking

Record **Restore** **Splits** **1-Line**   **Ending Balance:**   3,225.24

Figure 9.2 After editing the date and payment for check 1201

Tip

When a transaction is selected, pressing Alt+Backspace, the shortcut for the Edit Undo command, cancels the last change you made. Clicking on Restore cancels all changes you made to the transaction and moves the cursor to the Date field in that transaction.

Your register should now look like Figure 9.2. Notice how Quicken adjusts all balances and entries to reflect the changes to check 1201. The Ending Balance is now $3,225.24. Since the date 8/15 made check 1201 a postdated transaction, the new date of 8/5 causes this check to move before check 1202.

Voiding a Transaction

Voiding keeps everything in a transaction intact except the amount, which Quicken changes to 0. In effect, this works the same as when you void a check or deposit in your paper check register. As an exercise, let's void check 1202 to American Express in Figure 9.2 (or void one of your own transactions):

1. Click on any **check 1202 field** to select this transaction.
2. Press **Ctrl+V**, the shortcut for the Edit Void Transaction command.
3. Click on **Record** to confirm.

Notice in Figure 9.3 how Quicken changes the Payment amount of check 1202 from 225.62 to 0, inserts *VOID* before the payee name "American Express" in the Description field, and makes reconciling easier by inserting an X in the C (Cleared) field indicating that the check has cleared. What's more, Quicken automatically recalculates all balances to reflect the voided check so that the Ending Balance in the bottom right corner is now $3,450.86.

		Bank Account: Checking					
M/D Year	Num	Payee Memo Category	Payment	C	Deposit	Balance	
8/5 1992	1199	Coast Savings and Loan August payment Auto:Loan	325 64			4,474 36	
8/5 1992	1200	Home Mortgage of America August payment Housing	923 50			3,550 86	
8/5 1992	DEP	Deposit Bond Int 6/30 Invest Inc			250 00	3,800 86	
8/5 1992	1201	MidCounty Insurance Car insurance 6 months Insurance	350 00			3,450 86	
8/5 1992	1202	**VOID**American Express Includes credit of 125 Entertain		x		3,450 86	
8/10 1992	Num	Payee Memo Category	Payment		Deposit		

Record	Restore	Splits	1-Line		Ending Balance:	3,450.86

Figure 9.3 Voiding check 1202

If you void a transaction that transfers money between accounts, such as a transfer from a savings account to a checking account, voiding the transaction in one account automatically voids it in the second account. (Performing a transfer transaction is discussed in Lesson 26).

Deleting a Transaction

Deleting a transaction not only deletes it from a register but also deletes it from the QDATA file on disk. To see how this works, first enter a transaction such as check 1203 for 85.20 to PG+E shown in Figure 9.4. Now let's delete it:

1. Select **check 1203** by clicking on any field in this transaction.
2. Delete the transaction by pressing **Ctrl+D**, the shortcut for the Edit Delete Transaction command. You'll see the dialog box shown in Figure 9.4 confirming that you really want to delete the transaction.
3. Click on **Yes** to complete the deletion. (Click on No to cancel the deletion and leave the selected transaction intact.) Quicken deletes check 1203 and automatically recalculates all balances to reflect the deleted check. The Ending Balance is again $3,450.86.

Tip
To protect transactions from being accidentally deleted or changed, assign a password to them.

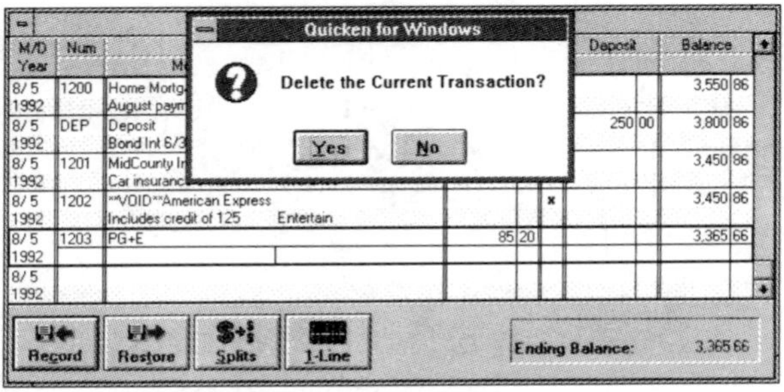

Figure 9.4   Deleting a transaction

Because Quicken "memorizes" transactions you've entered, a deleted transaction isn't gone for good. If, for example, you now enter a new transaction and type **PG+** in the Description field, Quicken finishes **PG+E** for you. (Memorized transactions are discussed in Lesson 19.)

♦ *Lesson* ♦

10

Locating Transactions

Finding Related Transactions

In Quicken, you can use the Edit Find command to quickly search for and locate specific types of transactions in a register or in a Write Checks window. Suppose you want to find each check written to American Express. Here's how to do this or to search for your own transactions:

1. To follow along with this example, first enter all transactions in Figure 10.1 from check 1203 on.
2. Decide at what point you want to start the search and position the cursor there. In Figure 10.1, the cursor is positioned in the 8/5 Deposit transaction.
3. Click on ▲ in the IconBar or press **Ctrl+F**, shortcuts for the Edit Find command. You'll see the Find Transaction window shown in Figure 10.1.

		Bank Account: Checking					
M/D Year	Num	Payee / Memo / Category	Payment	Clr	Deposit	Balance	
8/ 5 1992	DEP	Deposit / Bond Int 6/30 Invest Inc			250 00	3,800 86	
8/ 5 1992	1201	MidCounty Insurance / Car insurance 6 months Insurance	350 00			3,450 86	
8/ 5 1992	1202	**VOID**American Express / Includes credit of 125 Entertain		x		3,450 86	
8/ 6 1992	1203	American Express / Incudes credit of 125 Entertain	325 50			3,125 36	
8/ 6 1992	DEP	Deposit / My 7/31 paycheck Salary			1,545 36	4,670 72	
8/ 6 1992	1204	Carol Bright / Babysitting Childcare					

			Find	
		Find	American Express	
		Search	Payee ⬧ Match if Contains ⬧	
			Previous Next	

Record   Restore   Splits   1-Line

Figure 10.1 Setting up a search

Tip

Because the Find transaction window is a window and not a dialog box, you can minimize, move, close, or stack it just like other windows.

4. In the Find text box, type the text or value you want to find. In this case, type **American Express**.

Tip

If you accept the Match If default of Contains the search won't be case-sensitive and you can enter your Find text in either upper- or lowercase. To make a search case-sensitive, set Match If to Exact.

5. If you want, limit the search. For example, to limit the search from the default of All Fields to just the Payee field, open the Search drop-down list by clicking on the Search arrow ⬧ . In the

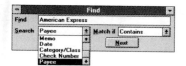

Figure 10.2   Limiting the search

drop-down list shown in Figure 10.2, click on Payee.

Note: The Search drop-down list contains most fields that make up a register transaction with two exceptions: Amount represents both the Payment and Deposit fields, so you aren't able to search either of these fields exclusively. There also isn't a selection for the Balance field; only the All Fields selection searches this field (as well as all other fields in the register).

6. You can further refine the search by limiting what Quicken considers to be a "match." In this case, the Match If default of Contains means that Quicken will find a transaction if the Payee field in any way contains the Find string "American Express". Although we'll accept this default for the purposes of this exercise, open the Match If drop-down list by clicking on the Match arrow ▣ to see the options shown in Figure 10.3.

Note: The Match If options, Greater, Greater or Equal, Less, and Less or Equal work with values only. All other options will find value or text,

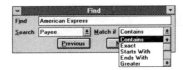

Figure 10.3 Limiting what is a match

depending on the Find string you use. For example, setting Match If to Starts With and Find as Ex will find Exp and Expense; using a Find of 3 will find 3 and 35. The Exact option, on the other hand, only finds something that exactly and completely matches, including case and blank spaces.

7. Begin the search by clicking on **Next**. Starting from the position of the cursor, Quicken searches the Payee field of each subsequent transaction. Since Match If is set to Contains, Quicken finds the first match in check 1202 and moves the cursor to its Payee field as

M/D Year	Num	Payee / Memo	Category	Payment	Clr	Deposit	Balance	
		Bank Account: Checking						
8/5 1992	DEP	Deposit Bond Int 6/30	Invest Inc			250 00	3,800 86	
8/5 1992	1201	MidCounty Insurance Car insurance 6 months	Insurance	350 00			3,450 86	
8/5 1992	1202	**VOID**American Express Includes credit of 125	Entertain		x		3,450 86	
8/6 1992	1203	American Express Incudes credit of 125	Entertain	325 50			3,125 36	
8/6 1992	DEP	Deposit My 7/31 paycheck	Salary			1,545 36	4,670 72	
8/6 1992	1204	Carol Bright Babysitting	Childcare					

Record   Restore   Splits   1-Li

Find	American Express
Search	Payee	Match if	Contains

Previous   Next

Figure 10.4 The first match Quicken finds

shown in Figure 10.4. You now ' tions: To continue the search, cl. end the search, double-click on th **Transaction** window control box ▣ ; to mak changes to check 1202 before continuing the search, click on the **Find Transaction Mini- mize** button ▣ . Then make whatever changes you want. To resume the search, double-click on at the bottom of your screen to reopen the Find Transaction window. Then click on **Next** to resume the search.

Tip

If you see the "No matching transactions were found" message at this point and you think there should be a match, check your Find Trans- action settings, especially the spelling in the Find text box. If you've set Match If to Exact, try setting it to Contains. This will help if your Find text isn't identical to its entry form. For exam- ple, if what you're looking includes a blank space at the end, Exact won't consider it a match to your Find text but Contains will.

8. Click on **Next** to continue the search; Quicken moves to the Payee field of the next match it finds, in this case, check 1203.

Tip

If you click on Previous at this point in the search, the cursor moves back to the prior match, check 1202.

9. Click on **Next** again to resume the search. Because Quicken doesn't find any more matches after check 1202, you'll see a message asking you if you want to continue the search starting at the beginning of the register.

10. Click on **No** to end the search. Then double-click on the **Find Transaction window** control box to close this window.

Tip
You can find transactions in a specific field that don't include an entry by searching for =~. For example, entering =~ in the Find text box and setting Search to Category/Class would find any transaction missing a Category entry.

11

Printing a Register

Directing a Register to a Printer

Once you create a register, you'll probably want to print a hard copy of it. In fact, it's a good idea to always keep a paper copy of a register on hand so that if disaster ever strikes and you lose your QDATA file, you at least will have a record of what you've done.

To print a copy of the register shown at the end of Lesson 10, or to print a register containing your own transactions:

1. Make sure the register is the active window, then click on  in the IconBar or press **Ctrl+P**. Both are shortcuts for the File Print Register command. You'll see the dialog box shown in Figure 11.1.

2. Specify print transaction dates that reflect the transactions you want to print. The default settings in this case, 1/1/92 to 8/6/92, represent the first day of the current year to the date of the last transaction. To print only the August transac-

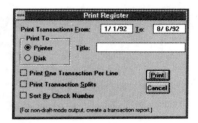

Figure 11.1   The Print Register
dialog box

tions, type **8/1/92** in the first text box. (Remember that you can also use + and – to change the date in a date text box.)
3. Accept the Print to default, **Printer**. This setting prints to your printer in *draft-mode*.

Quicken only allows you to print a register in draft mode. This means that you really can't customize it like other reports. For example, you can use the File Select Printer command to change the orientation to landscape (a good way to print long Payee names) but any fonts you assign won't be used. (These settings are discussed in Lesson 32.) To create a custom register report, use the Reports Custom Transaction command instead.

4. If you want, click on the **Title** text box and add an identifying title up to 36 characters. For instance, to add the title shown in Figure 11.2, type **Coast Savings 116394**.

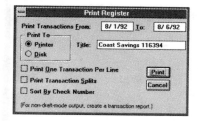

Figure 11.2 Changing the Print Register settings

➡️ **Note:** If you don't include a title, Quicken adds one, such as "Check Register," to identify the type of account. What's more Quicken always adds the account name, "Checking" in this case, on each page regardless of whose title you use.

5. To print the register, click on **Print**. While Quicken is printing you'll see a message indicating where the register is being printed. Click on **Cancel** at any time to cancel printing.

You can see the result in Figure 11.3. The transactions are printed in the order they appear in the register. Each transaction is printed on two lines unless it contains a category; then it's printed on three lines.

At the top of every page of the register, Quicken includes a title, the page number, the name of the account, and the date the register is printed. Figure 11.3, then, shows page 1 of the Checking register, which was printed on 8/10/92. The custom title, Coast

```
                          Coast Savings 116394
Checking                                                    Page 1
8/10/92
Date   Num           Transaction            Payment  C  Deposit   Balance
-------------------------------------------------------------------------
8/ 1         Opening Balance                        x  5,000.00  5,000.00
1992 memo:
        cat: [Checking]

8/ 3 ATM     ATM Cash withdrawal             200.00            4,800.00
1992 memo:
        cat: Misc

8/ 5 1199    Coast Savings and Loan          325.64            4,474.36
1992 memo:   August payment
        cat: Auto:Loan

8/ 5 1200    Home Mortgage of America        923.50            3,550.86
1992 memo:   August payment
        cat: Housing

8/ 5 DEP     Deposit                                    250.00 3,800.86
1992 memo:   Bond Int 6/30
        cat: Invest Inc

8/ 5 1201    MidCounty Insurance             350.00            3,450.86
1992 memo:   Car insurance 6 months
        cat: Insurance

8/ 5 1202    **VOID**American Express            x          3,450.86
1992 memo:   Includes credit of 125
        cat: Entertain

8/ 6 1203    American Express                325.50            3,125.36
1992 memo:   Incudes credit of 125
        cat: Entertain

8/ 6 DEP     Deposit                               1,545.36 4,670.72
1992 memo:   My 7/31 paycheck
        cat: Salary

8/ 6 1204    Carol Bright                     25.00            4,645.72
1992 memo:   Babysitting
        cat: Childcare
```

Figure 11.3   The printed check register

Savings 116394, appears at the top of each page of the register. If you don't include a title, Quicken adds a descriptive one of its own.

Print Register Options

Three options are included in the Print Register dialog box that you may want to use:

- **Print one transaction per line** prints each transaction on one line rather than three. Quicken limits the Payee field to 22 characters and both the Memo and Category fields to 15 characters each.
- **Print transaction splits** allows you to print each of the categories to which a split transaction is allocated. (Splitting a transaction is discussed in Lesson 24.)

- **Sort by check number** first prints by date all transactions that do not include check numbers. Then, all transactions with check numbers are printed in ascending order. Any missing checks are denoted by *. When checks are sorted by check number, Quicken does *not* print the Balance column.

12

The Reconciliation Process: Entering Bank Statement Information

The Reconciliation Process

One you begin using Quicken for your checking account, you'll want to reconcile the register against your bank statement. The basic procedure is the same as when you reconcile a paper check register. The difference, though, is that it's actually easier to do this in Quicken because the calculations are done for you.

Quicken takes the traditional reconciliation process and separates it into five steps:

- Provide bank statement information to Quicken.
- Mark cleared transactions.
- Determine if any difference exists between the adjusted register balance and the ending bank statement balance.
- Make a final adjustment.
- Print a reconciliation report.

Each of these steps is covered in the next three lessons.

Tip
It's best to reconcile a register each month in Quicken, just like you frequently do in a paper check register.

Entering Bank Statement Information

In Quicken, the first step in the reconciliation process is to enter some information from your bank statement. To see how this works, let's suppose that you just received a bank statement ending 8/7/92 for the checking account shown in Figure 12.1. The beginning balance is $5,000; the ending balance is $4,243.97 A

M/D Year	Num	Payee / Memo / Category	Payment	Clr	Deposit	Balance
8/6 1992	1204	Carol Bright / Babysitting / Childcare	25 00			4,645 72
8/6 1992	1205	Larry Yen / Dentist for Martie / Medical	240 50			4,405 22
8/6 1992	1206	Phone / For July / Telephone	125 65			4,279 57
8/6 1992	ATM	ATM Cash withdrawal / 100Ent,50 Gas, 50 Clean / Misc	100 00			4,179 57
8/6 1992	1207	Safeway / Mom's visit / Groceries	150 45			4,029 12
8/6 1992						

Bank Account: Checking

Record   Restore   Splits   1-Line   Ending Balance: 4,029 12

Figure 12.1 The checking account to be reconciled

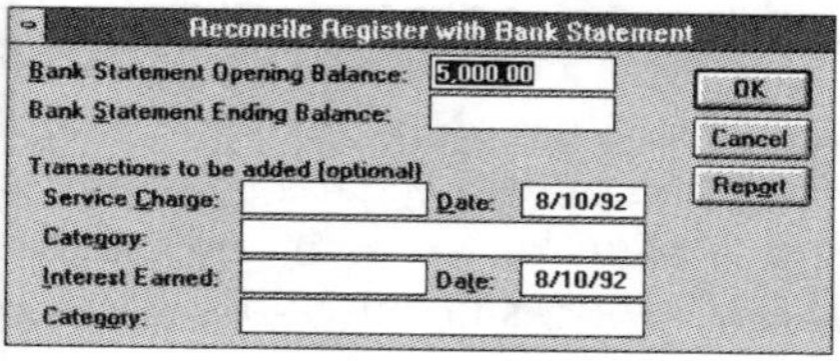

Figure 12.2 Beginning the reconciliation

service charge of $20 is assessed; interest earned on the balance is $8.63.

To follow along with this exercise, take a moment and enter the new 8/6 transactions shown in Figure 12.1: the $100 ATM withdrawal and checks 1205 through 1207. To enter this bank statement information (or information of your own) and begin the reconciliation process:

1. With the check register open and active, click on ⊞ in the IconBar, the shortcut for the Activities Reconcile command. You'll see the dialog box shown in Figure 12.2. The Bank Statement Opening Balance of $5,000 represents all transactions in the register marked cleared (* or x). If you haven't reconciled an account before, this amount equals the beginning account balance, since it is the only transaction marked cleared.

2. Verify that the beginning balance on your bank statement equals the Bank Statement Opening Balance. In this example, both equal $5,000. If these balances don't match, you first need to make sure that they do. Press **Tab** to move to the Bank Statement Ending Balance or click on this text box.

Tip

If these balances don't match, first make sure that they occur on the same date. If so, then check the bank statement to see if any checks, withdrawals, and deposits not included in your Quicken register recently cleared.

3. In the Bank Statement Ending Balance text box, enter the ending balance shown on the bank statement without a dollar sign. In this example, type **4243.97**.

4. If you have *not* entered the service charge as a transaction in the register, press **Tab** to move to the Service Charge text box. Then enter the amount of the service charge without a dollar sign; in this case, type **20**. Next, press **Tab** to move to the date text box. Type the date the service charge occurred, **8/7/92**, or keep pressing – until the date you want appears.

5. If you want to assign a category to the service charge, press **Tab** to move to the Category text box. Then press **Ctrl+C** or click on in the IconBar to access the Category & Transfer List window. Next, scroll through this list and double-click on Bank Chrg so that Quicken enters this category into the text box.

Tip

When you have entered all the service charge information, Quicken automatically enters a cleared transaction for the service charge in the register even though you haven't confirmed these settings by clicking on OK. (You'll see this transaction in Lesson 13.)

6. If your account is interest bearing, and you have *not* entered the interest as a transaction in the register, press **Tab** to move to the Interest Earned text box. Then enter the amount of the interest without a dollar sign. Here, type **8.63**. Next, press **Tab** to move to the date text box. Enter the date the interest occurred, **8/7/92** in this case.

7. If you want, press **Tab** to move to the Category text box. Since the Category & Transfer List window should still be open, click anywhere within this window to activate it. Then scroll until you find Int Inc and double-click on this category. Double-click on the **Category & Transfer List window** control box 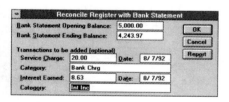 to close this window. At this point, the dialog box should look like Figure 12.3.

Figure 12.3   Entering information for a reconciliation

Tip

Like the service charge, Quicken automatically enters the interest earned as a cleared transaction. (You can see the corresponding register transaction in Lesson 13.)

---

8. Click on any of these three buttons:

- **OK** to confirm this information and continue the reconciliation process. You'll now see the Reconcile window, discussed next in Lesson 13.
- **Cancel** to cancel the reconciliation. Remember though, that any service charge and interest earned have already been entered as cleared transactions in the register and won't be cancelled.
- **Report** to create two types of reconciliation reports. (See Lesson 15.)

13

The Reconciliation Process: Working in the Reconcile Window

What is the Reconcile Window?

After you finish entering the bank statement information in Lesson 12 and click on OK, you'll see the Reconcile window shown in Figure 13.1.

Initially, the Reconcile window lists all transactions *not* currently cleared in the register. Notice that check 1202 doesn't appear, because in Lesson 9, this check was voided and marked as cleared. But, two cleared (✔) transactions do appear: the service charge and interest earned amounts entered in the Reconcile Register with Bank Statement dialog box in Lesson 12.

Transactions are sorted as follows in the Reconcile window: Deposits appear first, sorted by date; then all withdrawals that aren't checks, sorted by date; and finally, checks, sorted by check number.

The Reconcile window is designed to make balancing your account easier. It's more efficient to use this window to mark transactions as cleared rather than

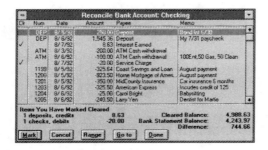

Figure 13.1   The Reconcile window

doing so in the register, and any transactions you mark as cleared here are automatically updated in the register.

⇨ **Note:**   Because this is a window and not a dialog box, you can minimize, move, close, and stack it just like other windows. You can't, however, resize it. You can't, for instance, increase the window size to display the Category field for each transaction—it isn't included in a Reconcile window.

The most important information appears on the right side of the Reconcile window where Quicken keeps track of any adjustments you make. The Bank Statement Balance of $4,243.97 is the ending bank statement amount you entered in Lesson 12. The Cleared Balance of $4,988.63 represents the total of all cleared transactions in the register. Since this is the first time the Checking register is being reconciled, $4,988.63 equals the $5,000 opening balance plus the cleared tally on the left side of the window—the $8.63 interest earned less the $20 service charge.

The Difference of $744.66 equals the Cleared Balance less the Bank Statement Balance. In other words, it's the amount by which the two do *not* reconcile. When the Difference is 0, the adjusted register balance and the ending bank statement balance match and the accounts are reconciled.

Marking Cleared Transactions

Let's use the Reconcile window to mark the cleared transactions as well as make any necessary adjustments. In this example, let's assume that the bank statement lists deposits of $250 and $1,545.36; two $200 ATM withdrawals; all checks between 1199 and 1207 as cleared except 1202, 1205, and 1206; and an automatic payment of $40. Remember, the $20 service charge and $8.63 interest earned have already been entered and cleared in Lesson 12.

Tip
It helps to also keep track of what you're doing in the bank statement by manually placing a checkmark next to each transaction you mark as cleared in Quicken. That way, you can find any transactions that don't appear in the register.

The steps to mark these, or transactions of your own, as cleared are:

1. On the bank statement, make sure that the first transaction—the $250 deposit—has cleared and is for exactly the same amount. In the Register window, click anywhere on this transaction and

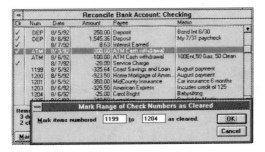

Figure 13.2   Marking a range of cleared checks

you will see how Quicken enters a ✔ in this deposit's Clr field. This transaction is now reflected in the deposit tally and Cleared Balance at the bottom of the window (Figure 13.2).

2. Check to make sure that the $1,545.36 deposit on 8/6 and the $200 ATM deposit on 8/3 have cleared on the bank statement. Then click on each to mark them as cleared. (We'll get to the second (incorrect) ATM deposit of $100 in a minute.)

3. Checks 1199 through 1204 have all cleared, so you can mark them all at once as a range. First, make sure that each amount matches the bank statement. Then click on **Range** to open the dialog box shown at the bottom of Figure 13.2. Type the lowest check number—**1199**—in the first text box, press **Tab** or click on the second text box, and then type the highest check in this range **1204**. When you click on **OK**, you'll see the message "Marking transactions" while Quicken does this work for you. Figure 13.3

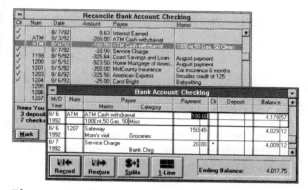

Figure 13.3 Going to a transaction from the Reconcile window

shows how Quicken marks all these checks as cleared.

> ### *Tip*
> You can include previously cleared checks in your check range. Notice that check 1202 doesn't appear in the Reconcile window, indicating either it has cleared or been voided.

4. View any remaining uncleared checks by using the scroll bar or pressing ↓. Then click on check 1207 to mark it as cleared.

If you incorrectly mark a transaction as cleared, use the same technique to reverse the action as you did to clear it. Clicking on a transaction marks it as cleared; clicking on that same transaction deletes the cleared ✔.

Changing an Incorrect Transaction

While you're reconciling, you may see an incorrect transaction, such as the $100 ATM withdrawal in Figure 13.3, which should be $200. To make the correction, you must move back to the register. The Reconcile window provides an easy way to do this:

1. Use the scroll bar or ↑ and ↓ to highlight the incorrect transaction, the 8/6 $100 ATM withdrawal.
2. Click on **Go To**. This opens and moves you to the correct register, as shown in Figure 13.3, where this transaction is already selected.
3. Make the adjustment to the transaction. In this case, keep pressing **Tab** until you reach the Payment field, and then type **200**. Click on **Record** to record this change.
4. Minimize the register window and return to the Reconcile window by clicking on the Checking register's minimize button, ▣ . In the Reconcile window, the edited transaction is now highlighted.
5. Click on this transaction to mark it as cleared. Figure 13.4 shows how the Reconcile window now appears.

Identifying and Entering Missing Transactions

At this point in the reconciliation process, it's time to stop and look at the Difference balance, which is 39.93 in Figure 13.4. Let's say that on the imaginary bank statement we've been working with, you were ticking

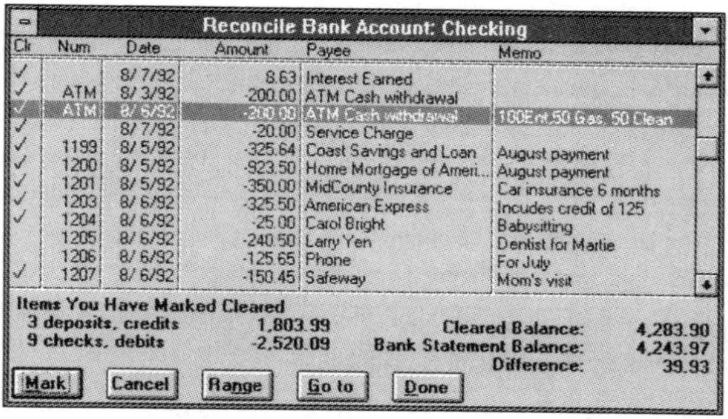

Figure 13.4 After clearing all transactions

off transactions marked as cleared in Quicken, and you now see a lone transaction not marked—a $40 automatic payment to the Y. It is not included in the Reconcile window, and must be treated as a missing transaction.

⇨ **Note:** If the Bank Statement Opening Balance in Lesson 12 differed from the beginning balance on the bank statement, then this Difference could potentially be a transaction incorrectly assumed as cleared.

To add a missing transaction, you must move back to the register and make this correction. To add the missing $40 payment (or a missing transaction of your own):

1. Move to the register window. If the register is already open, simply click anywhere on it. If it's minimized, double-click on its icon at the bot-

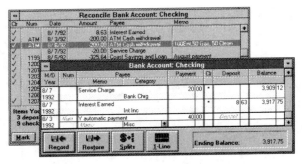

Figure 13.5 Adding a missing transaction

tom of the screen or click on the ▦ icon in the IconBar. Both the Reconcile window and Checking register will now be open (see Figure 13.5).

⚡ Don't close the Reconcile window or you'll disrupt the reconciliation process. Instead, minimize the Reconcile window by clicking on its Minimize button ▼. If you've already made the mistake and closed it, click on ⚖ to open the dialog box you first saw in Figure 12.2 of Lesson 12. Re-enter the Bank Statement Ending Balance—4243.96 in this case, but don't enter anything else. Click on OK, and you'll see the Reconcile window just as you left it.

2. Create a new transaction by pressing **Ctrl+N**, the shortcut for the Edit New Transaction command. In the Date field, keep pressing **Del** until the date displayed is erased. Then type the date of the transaction—**8/3/92** in this case. Press **Tab twice** to move to the Description field and type

Y automatic payment. Press **Tab** to move to the Payment field and type **40** or **40.00**. Press **Tab** twice and type **Misc** in the Category field. Click on **Record** to record this transaction.

3. Minimize the Checking register window and move back to the Reconcile window by clicking on the register's Minimize button, [▼]. As you can see in Figure 13.6, the $40 Y automatic payment transaction is now included and highlighted in the Reconcile window. Click on this transaction to mark it as cleared.

At this point, the reconciliation is virtually done. In Figure 13.6, all of the cleared transactions are marked, any incorrect transactions are fixed, and any missing transactions have been added. There's one more step before you complete the reconciliation—evaluating the Difference—and that's discussed next in Lesson 14.

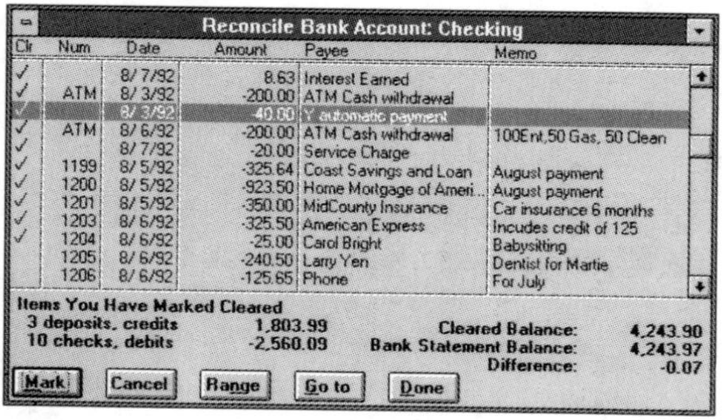

Figure 13.6 Evaluating the difference after clearing all transactions

◆ *Lesson* ◆

14

The Reconciliation Process: Completing the Reconciliation

Evaluating the Difference

The Difference at the bottom of the Reconcile window indicates the amount the reconciled balance in the register differs from the ending balance on the bank statement. Here's what you should do, depending on the Difference:

- If the Difference is 0, the two balances match and you can complete the reconciliation. Go on to "Completing the Reconciliation" in this lesson.
- If the Difference is small (less than $1 or $2, for example), you may just want to be done with it and have Quicken make the final adjustment. Go on to "Completing the Reconciliation" and let Quicken create a balance adjustment transaction.
- If the Difference is material to you ($2 or more, perhaps), there are still some remaining problems with the reconciliation. Go to "When the Difference Isn't 0: Common Reconciliation Errors."

When the Difference Isn't 0: Common Reconciliation Errors

If the Difference you are left with in the Reconcile window is material—greater than $2, for example—you haven't fully completed the reconciliation. Assuming that you started with a balance that corresponded to your beginning bank statement balance, the problem exists in the current reconciliation.

One way to zero in on the problem is to count the number of deposits and credits (checks, ATM withdrawals, and automatic payments) in the bank statement, and then compare them to the number of deposits and checks (withdrawals) at the bottom left of the Reconcile window. If they don't match, look for one or more of these problems:

- A transaction cleared in the bank statement that is still open in the Reconcile window.
- An open transaction that has been marked as cleared in the Reconcile window.
- A transaction cleared in the bank statement that is missing in the register.
- A service charge or interest earned that is entered and cleared more than once or not entered at all.

If the Difference still exists, here are some other things that may be causing the problem:

- A payment entered as a deposit, or vice versa.
- An amount is incorrectly entered, for example, 923 as 932.
- There may be a mistake in the bank statement.

At this point, you have a few options. By far the best thing to do is to find the problem yourself, then make the adjustment that corrects this. (If the adjustment is a transaction, remember to mark it as cleared.)

If you want to continue hunting for the problem at a later Quicken session, click on Close in the Reconcile window. To resume the reconciliation at a later date, select ⚖ in the IconBar. You'll then have to reenter the Bank Statement Ending Balance. Be aware, however, that if you've entered other transactions in the meantime they'll appear in the Reconcile window.

The final alternative is to complete the reconciliation and let Quicken make a final adjustment transaction for you. Although this may be the easiest thing to do, you may only be prolonging the problem in future reconciliations if the Difference stems from open (uncleared) transactions.

Completing the Reconciliation

Here's how to complete a reconciliation, such as the reconciliation we've been working on in Lesson 13 or one for your own bank statement:

1. In the Reconcile window, click on **Done**. If the Difference is $0.00, you'll see a congratulatory dialog box; go on to Step 3. If the Difference isn't 0, you'll see the Adjust Balance dialog box shown in Figure 14.1 telling you the current Difference——$0.07 in this case.

2. If the Difference is minimal, such as –$0.07 in this example, have Quicken make the adjustment transaction. First, type the date of the bank statement in the date text box—**8/7/92** in this case. Click on **Adjust Balance** to have Quicken make the adjustment transaction shown in Figure 14.2.

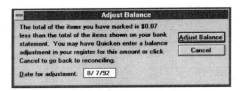

Figure 14.1 The dialog box when the Difference is not $0.00

Be aware that you won't see this transaction unless the register is already open.

3. You'll now see a dialog box informing you the reconciliation is complete; either click on **No** to complete the reconciliation without printing any reports or click on **Yes** to continue on and print the reports discussed next in Lesson 15.

Regardless of whether you choose Yes or No, the reconciliation is now complete and set up for the next time. If you clicked on ▣ in the IconBar now, the $4,243.97 Ending Bank Balance would appear in the dialog box you see as the Bank Statement Opening Balance. What's more, none of the transactions you just cleared will appear in the Reconcile window—they are now part of the Cleared Balance amount.

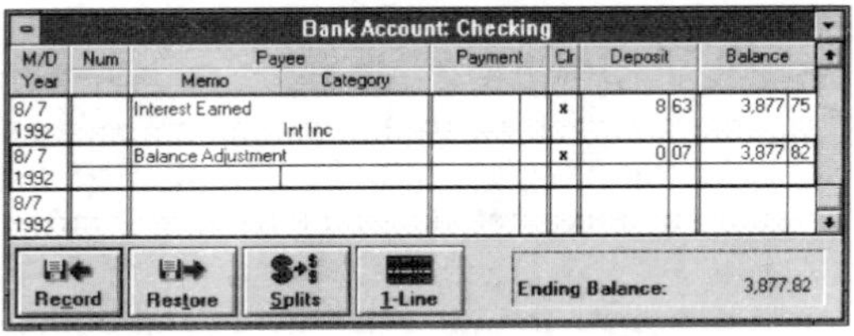

M/D Year	Num	Payee Memo Category	Payment	Clr	Deposit	Balance
8/7 1992		Interest Earned Int Inc		x	8 63	3,877 75
8/7 1992		Balance Adjustment		x	0 07	3,877 82
8/7 1992						

Record   Restore   Splits   1-Line   Ending Balance: 3,877.82

Figure 14.2 Quicken adjusting a balance

15

The Reconciliation Process: Printing Reconciliation Reports

Printing a Reconciliation Report

If you choose Yes in the Reconciliation Complete: Balance Adjusted dialog box after completing a reconciliation, you'll access the dialog box shown in Figure 15.1. From here, you can print two types of reconciliation reports.

To print a reconciliation report to a printer:

1. Accept the Print to default, **Printer**.
2. If you want to add a title of 36 characters or fewer, click on the **Report Title** text box, and type in the text. If you don't include a title, Quicken adds "Reconciliation Summary" on each page. Press **Tab** to move to the date text box.
3. In the date text box, change the current date—8/10/92—to the bank statement date. In this example, you'd type **8/7/92**. (In a report, this date

appears after text like "Register Balance as of" and
"Uncleared Transaction Detail Up To:")

4. Choose the report type. Either accept the default,
   Summary and Uncleared or click on the radio
   button.

5. Click on **Print** to begin printing. While Quicken
   is printing, you'll see a message indicating where
   the register is being printed. When Quicken is
   finished printing, it closes this dialog box and
   returns you to the register, if it is open.

If you choose not to print reconciliation reports at
the end of the reconciliation process, or you would like
to print a second report, you can still do so during your
current Quicken session. Click on ▨ in the IconBar to
access the Reconcile Register with Bank Statement dialog box first shown in Lesson 12. (Don't worry that the
new opening balance is the ending balance after the
reconciliation.) Then click on Report to access the dialog box shown in Figure 15.1. In fact, you can continue
to print reconciliation reports until you perform the
next reconciliation. If you've entered other register

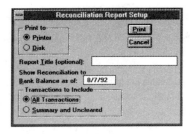

Figure 15.1   Printing a report

transactions in the meantime, however, they'll appear in the uncleared transaction portions of the reports.

The All Transactions Report

The All Transactions report creates a four-page print-out. The first page provides a summary of the reconciliation. The remaining three pages provide detailed information about the summary data.

The "Bank Statement—Cleared Transactions" portion shows the number and amount of payments and deposits that created the ending bank balance, called Ending Balance of Bank Statement here. In this case, 10 payments totalling –2560.09 and 4 deposits and other credits (income) totalling 1,804.06 cleared in this bank statement. When added to the previous (beginning) balance, the result is the 4,243.97 Ending Balance of Bank Statement. The "Cleared Transaction Detail" on page 2 provides detail about these cleared transactions.

The "Your Records—Uncleared Transactions" portion reconciles the cleared (reconciled) register balance to the ending register balance. In Figure 15.2, for instance, the Cleared (reconciled) Balance is 4,243.97— the same amount as the Ending Balance of Bank Statement, above. This balance, less the uncleared transactions totalling –366.15, result in the Register Balance on 8/7/92 of 3,877.82. Page 3 provides a detailed "Uncleared Transaction Detail Up To 8/7/92" listing these uncleared transactions.

Since no transactions were entered in the register after the 8/7/92 reconciliation date, the Register Ending Balance is also 3,877.82. If later transactions were

```
                            Reconciliation Report
Checking                                                               Page 1
8/10/92                 RECONCILIATION SUMMARY



        BANK STATEMENT -- CLEARED TRANSACTIONS:

            Previous Balance:                                    4,243.90
                                                                 ------------
                Checks and Payments:            0 Items              0.00
                Deposits and Other Credits:     1 Item               0.07
                                                                 ------------
            Ending Balance of Bank Statement:                    4,243.97

        YOUR RECORDS -- UNCLEARED TRANSACTIONS:

            Cleared Balance:                                     4,243.97
                                                                 ------------
                Checks and Payments:            2 Items           -366.15
                Deposits and Other Credits:     0 Items              0.00
                                                                 ------------
            Register Balance as of  8/ 7/92:                     3,877.82
                                                                 ------------
                Checks and Payments:            0 Items              0.00
                Deposits and Other Credits:     0 Items              0.00
                                                                 ------------
            Register Ending Balance:                             3,877.82
```

```
                            Reconciliation Report
Checking                                                               Page 2
8/10/92                 CLEARED TRANSACTION DETAIL


  Date    Num      Payee          Memo        Category    Clr   Amount
-------- ----- --------------- --------------- --------------- --- -----------

Cleared Checks and Payments
                                                                 -----------
Total Cleared Checks and Payments             0 Items              0.00

Cleared Deposits and Other Credits
  8/ 7/92        Balance Adjustme                            x     0.07
                                                                 -----------
Total Cleared Deposits and Other Credits      1 Item              0.07

                                                                 ===========
Total Cleared Transactions                    1 Item              0.07
```

Figure 15.2 A printed Reconciliation Report
(pages 1 and 2)

```
                                  Reconciliation Report
Checking
8/10/92                                                              Page 3
                      UNCLEARED TRANSACTION DETAIL UP TO  8/ 7/92

   Date    Num        Payee          Memo           Category   Clr   Amount
 --------  -----  ---------------  ---------------  ---------------  ---  -----------

Uncleared Checks and Payments

  8/ 6/92 1205  Larry Yen      Dentist for Mar Medical             -240.50
  8/ 6/92 1206  Phone          For July        Telephone           -125.65
                                                                   -----------
 Total Uncleared Checks and Payments            2 Items             -366.15

Uncleared Deposits and Other Credits
                                                                   -----------
 Total Uncleared Deposits and Other Credits     0 Items                0.00

 Total Uncleared Transactions                   2 Items            ===========
                                                                    -366.15
```

```
                                  Reconciliation Report
Checking
8/10/92                                                              Page 4
                      UNCLEARED TRANSACTION DETAIL AFTER  8/ 7/92

   Date    Num        Payee          Memo           Category   Clr   Amount
 --------  -----  ---------------  ---------------  ---------------  ---  -----------

Uncleared Checks and Payments
                                                                   -----------
 Total Uncleared Checks and Payments            0 Items                0.00

Uncleared Deposits and Other Credits
                                                                   -----------
 Total Uncleared Deposits and Other Credits     0 Items                0.00

 Total Uncleared Transactions                   0 Items            ===========
                                                                       0.00
```

Figure 15.2 A printed Reconciliation Report (pages 3 and 4)

present, however, then these would be included and would create a different Register Ending Balance. Page 4 provides a listing of "Uncleared Transaction Detail After 8/7/92."

The Summary and Uncleared Report

The Summary and Uncleared Report is made up of two pages: a reconciliation summary on Page 1 and un-cleared transactions detail on Page 2. In fact, this report provides the same information you see on Pages 1 and 3 of the All Transactions report shown in Figure 15.2.

Tip

If text in a Reconciliation Report is truncated, try printing the report sideways (landscape) or changing the font. (See Lesson 32.)

◆ *Lesson* ◆

16
Writing Checks

The Check Writing Process

The Write Checks window, shown in Figure 16.1, enables you to enter bank account transactions merely by writing checks. You should feel right at home in the Write Checks window, because it resembles a paper checkbook—each blank check has fields for the date, amount, payee, and the like.

 Although you can write checks in Quicken at any time, you can't print them unless you have preprinted checks from Intuit. (See Lesson 17.)

Filling Out a Check

Filling out a check in the Write Checks window works almost the same as entering a transaction in a register window; all the same keystrokes and mouse actions apply. The only peculiar thing about writing checks is that no check numbers are used at this stage; in fact, the Write Checks window doesn't even show a check

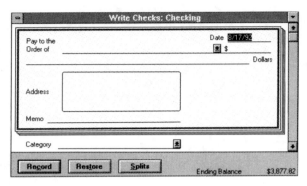

Figure 16.1   The Write Checks window

number. Check numbers aren't assigned until you actually print the checks.

Use the steps below to familiarize yourself with this process. Fill out a $1,550.60 check to the IRS for an estimated tax payment on 8/17/92 (or write a check for your own account):

1. Open the **Write Checks** window shown in Figure 16.1 by clicking on in the IconBar or pressing **Ctrl+W**, the shortcut for the Activities Write Checks command.

2. Enter the date of the transaction in the Date field. For the current example, type **8/17/92** in place of the current date that Quicken automatically supplies. (Remember that you can press + or – to increase or decrease the date.)

3. Type the payee name—in this exercise, **Internal Revenue Service**.

4. Enter the amount of the check in the $ field without any commas or dollar signs—for example, **1550.60**. When you press **Tab** or click on

the next field, Quicken automatically spells out
the amount in the line below.

5. If you plan to mail the check in a windowed
envelope, enter the payee name and address in
the Address field. You can enter up to five lines of
text, making sure to press **Enter** after each line.
To automatically copy the payee name you entered above, press ' or " in the first line of the
Address field.

6. If you want, click on the **Memo** field and then
type a memo such as **Estimated tax payment**.

7. If you want to enter a category, click on the
Category field. In this case, click on ▪ and select **Tax:Fed** from the drop-down list.

8. Click on **Record** to save this check. You'll now
see a new blank check in the window.

Viewing Checks in the Write Checks Window

If you've written more than one check, you can use the
keys listed in Lesson 7 to scroll through the Write
Checks window. For example, PgUp moves to the previous check.

Once you've printed a check, however, Quicken removes it from the Write Checks window. Then the only
place you can view the transaction is in the register.

Viewing Check Information in the Register

When you write a check in the Write Checks window,
Quicken also enters the corresponding transaction in

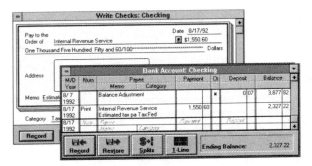

Figure 16.2   Check information in the check register

the register and updates the register balance. So, if you now click on ▦ in the IconBar or press Ctrl+R to open the Checking register in Figure 16.2, you'll see the IRS transaction.

Notice that Quicken uses "Print" for the check number in the Num field. This text will be replaced with an actual check number when you later print the check. (See Lesson 17.)

Editing, Deleting, and Voiding a Check

Checks are edited, voided, or deleted exactly like any other transaction, with one exception: You can do so in either the Write Checks window or the register window. The results are incorporated into both windows. (See Lesson 9.)

◆ *Lesson* ◆

17

Printing Checks

Ordering Checks

Before you can print checks in Quicken, you must obtain specially ordered checks from Intuit. The check catalog that accompanied your Quicken manual contains all the details. You *can* use checks from other sources, but only if they have exactly the same layout as Intuit checks. In addition, Intuit checks have numbers along their edges (near the tractor-feed holes) that are quite helpful for positioning continuous-feed checks.

There are two things to keep in mind when ordering checks:

- Dot-matrix printers require continuous-feed checks. Laser printers and inkjet printers have paper trays and therefore require page-oriented checks.

- Make sure your Quicken checks have much higher numbers than your personal checks. That way, you'll avoid duplicate check numbers, and you can easily differentiate your personal and

Quicken checks. (Having two sets of check numbers isn't a problem; the bank doesn't care what check numbers you use—they're for your records only.)

Printer Considerations

Normally, Quicken prints to the default Windows printer. Therefore, if you've had success printing from other Windows applications, you probably won't need to change your printer setup in Quicken. The one exception is if you're printing checks on a continuous-feed printer. Then you must change the printer's form height before printing checks. (If you have this type of printer, go to Lesson 18.)

Printing a Check from Your Account

Assuming you've created the check in Lesson 16, let's further assume that you have a laser printer using Standard checks. To print the sample check, or a different check:

 Tip
You can print a sample check whether or not you've entered a check in the Write Checks window. To do so, select the File Print Checks command and then click on Sample.

1. Insert your preprinted checks in your printer. For a page-oriented printer, insert the checks as you would letterhead. For a continuous-feed printer,

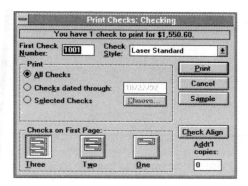

Figure 17.1 Print Checks: Checking
dialog box

insert the checks as you would any continuous
form.

2. Select the **File Print Checks** command.
Quicken displays the dialog box shown in Figure
17.1 for page-oriented printers (laser printers and
inkjet printers). If you have a continuous-feed
printer (a dot matrix printer) the dialog box
won't include buttons for controlling the number of checks on the first page or a text field for
additional copies.

3. Enter the number of your first preprinted
Quicken check. Let's assume the first check is
4000, so type **4000** in the First Check Number
text box.

4. Specify the type of checks you've ordered. In this
case, click on ◾ to open the Check Style drop-
down list and click on Laser Standard.

5. Click on **Print** to start printing. Quicken prints
the check shown in Figure 17.2.

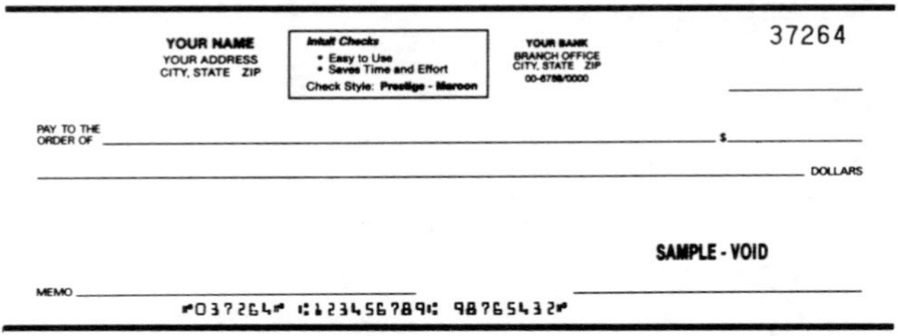

Figure 17.2   Printing a Standard Laser check

6. When you see the message asking you whether the check printed correctly, click on **Yes**. (If there was a problem—for example, the alignment wasn't correct on your continuous-feed printer, or the paper jammed—click on **No** to return to the Print Checks dialog box and try again.)

After printing a check, Quicken removes it from the Write Checks window. It also updates the check register to display the check number—in this example, 4000—in place of the word "Print.".

Setting Print Options

In the previous example, all the available checks (1 in this case) were printed. If you examine Figure 17.1 again, though, you'll see that you can also use the Print radio buttons to print checks based on date or print only selected checks.

The first option lets you print only those checks within a specified date range; for example, up to 8/10/92. Click on the Checks Dated Through radio button and type **8/10/92** in the text box to its right.

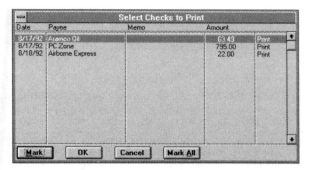

Figure 17.3 Selecting checks to print

The second option means you can identify, one by one, those checks you want printed. In this case, you would click on the Selected Checks radio button and then click on Choose. Figure 17.3 shows an example of the window that appears. Each check that has the word "Print" in the right-hand column is selected for printing. To deselect a check so that it isn't printed, double-click on it. If you later want to reselect it for printing, double-click on it again. When you're done, click on OK to return to the Print Checks dialog box. Now, when you click on Print, only the checks that you've marked will print.

Reprinting Checks

Quicken makes it easy to reprint a check. Let's again use the IRS check for this example:

1. If the Checking register isn't open, open it by clicking on 🖩 in the IconBar or pressing **Ctrl+R**.

2. Click on the **Num** field of the check you want to reprint—in this case, check 4000 to the IRS.

3. Choose **Print** from the drop-down list that automatically opens. Quicken instantly replaces the check number with "Print."

4. Click on **Record**. Quicken saves the new settings and creates a new copy of the check in the Write Checks window.

5. Now print the check as described in "Printing a Check From Your Account" above.

18

Modifying Printer Setup for Printing Checks

Setting Up a Continuous-Feed Printer

There are two steps necessary to set up a continuous-feed (also called a tractor-feed) printer before you'll be able to successfully print checks on it:

- Set the printer's paper height
- Check the printer alignment

Setting the Paper Height

When printing checks on a continuous-feed printer, the printer's paper height must correspond to the height of the checks you've purchased. For this example, let's suppose you want to print Wallet size checks on an Epson FX-850 printer connected to the LPT1 port.

1. Select the printer that Quicken should use for printing checks. Choose the **File Printer Setup**

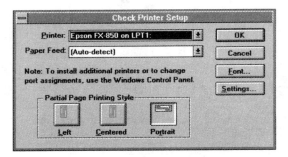

Figure 18.1   The Select Printer window

command and then select **Check Printer Setup** from the cascade menu. Figure 18.1 shows the window that appears. Click on ⬛ to open the Check Printer drop-down list. Then click on your printer, such as "Epson FX-850 on LPT1:" in this case.

⇨ **Note:** The initial entry you see in the Printer drop-down list is probably different from the one you see in Figure 18.1, depending on the printer(s) you have installed in Windows.

2. Make sure that the Paper Feed setting is correct for your printer. A setting of (**Auto-detect**) works correctly most of the time because Quicken reads the information it needs from the printer driver. Occasionally, however, Quicken makes the wrong choice—for example, when a dot matrix printer uses a paper tray. In this case, you'll need to click on ⬛ to open the drop-down list and then click on Page-oriented.

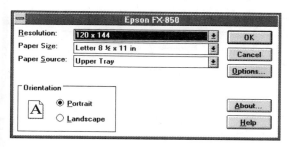

Figure 18.2 Printer-specific dialog box for the Epson FX-850

3. Change the check height in the printer-specific dialog box by clicking on **Settings**. Figure 18.2 shows the dialog box that appears for the Epson FX-850 (the dialog box for your printer is bound to differ). To change the check height in this dialog box, click on ⬛ to open the Paper Size drop-down list and then click on **User Defined Size** at the end of the list. (The dialog box for your printer probably has a similar setting.) You will then see a second dialog box, in which you can enter the height in inches—in this example, **2.83 inches** for Wallet size checks. (Table 18.1 shows the heights for all of Quicken's check types.)

⇨ **Note:** Some printer-specific dialog boxes request the paper size in the form of width and length. In this case, it's the length setting that corresponds to the check height.

4. Keep clicking on **OK** to exit all the printer-related dialog boxes.

Table 18.1   Check Height Settings

Check Type	Check Height
Standard	3.5 inches
Wallet	2.83 inches
Voucher	3.5 inches or 7.0 inches

Checking Printer Alignment

Another important aspect of printing on a continuous-feed printer is checking its alignment. To do so, you must print a sample check and then, if necessary, enter a setting that will correct the alignment. Here are the steps:

1. Assuming you've already completed the previous procedure to select the printer and set the check height, insert your Quicken checks into your printer as you would any continuous form.

2. Print a sample check. Select the **File Print Checks** command, and in the window that appears, click on **Sample**. Quicken displays a dialog box warning you not to adjust your printer after printing your check (you'll see why in a minute). When you click on OK, Quicken prints a test pattern on your printer and then displays the dialog box in Figure 18.3.

If you haven't set the page height before printing a sample check, Quicken will display a message indicating that the form size is too small for it to use its normal font size and that it will use the built-in printer font instead. If you see this message, make sure to set the check height, as described in the previous procedure.

3. If the vertical alignment is fine, just click OK. If not, enter a number that will correct the alignment. First, look at the test pattern. It includes a pointer line that looks like this:

```
<==== POINTER LINE ====== POINTER LINE ====== POINTER LINE ====>
```

This line points to one of the numbers in the perforated tractor strip along the side of the check. Enter the *even number* closest to the pointer line and click **OK**. Quicken prints another sample check taking into account the new alignment number you've supplied.

4. If the test pattern is still off vertically repeat step 3 until a sample prints correctly. (You'll have to make horizontal adjustments manually.)

When the test pattern prints correctly, note the number on the perforated tractor strip that lines up with a part of your printer. Then, the next time you

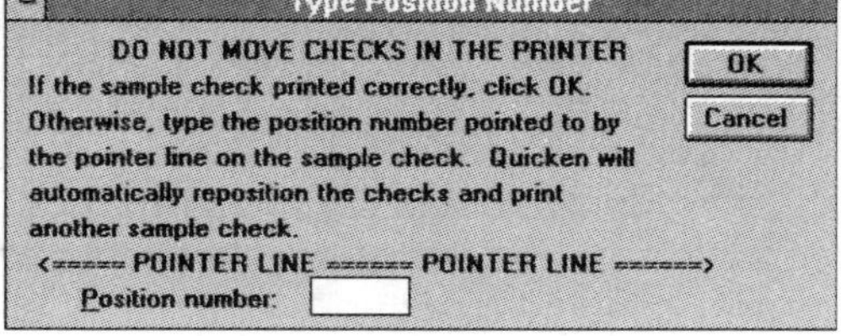

Figure 18.3 Correcting check alignment

print checks, line them up in the same way, so that you don't have to print a sample.

Now, go back to Lesson 17 and try printing a check from your account.

Page-Oriented Printer Considerations

Regular checks for page-oriented printers (laser printers, for instance) come three to a page. Therefore, when printing checks on these printers, you'll often wind up with a partial page of checks. (Voucher checks occupy a full page, you won't have a partial-page problem with these checks.) Rather than throw away the partial page, you can tell Quicken how many checks are included on it, and Quicken will use them.

Suppose you have a partial page with two checks that you'd like to print on a LaserJet III connected to LPT1 (or your own printer). What you need to do the next time you want to print checks from the Write Checks window is:

1. Select the printer that Quicken should use for printing checks. Choose the **Setup Check Printer Setup** command. When Quicken displays the window shown in Figure 18.1, click on ▓ to open the Check Printer drop-down list. Click on your printer, "**HP LaserJet III on LPT1**," in this case. Then click on **OK**.

2. Insert the partial page of checks in the printer's envelope feeder and the rest of the checks in the page tray as you would letterhead.

3. Select the **File Print Checks** command. Quicken displays the Print Checks window.

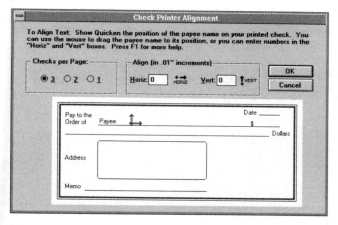

Figure 18.4   The Check Printer Alignment window

4. To tell Quicken how many checks are included on the partial page, click on one of the large buttons in the Checks on First Page group—in this example, the **Two** button.

5. At this point, you may need to adjust your printer alignment. To see if this is necessary, click on the **Check Align** button to access the window shown in Figure 18.4. Then press **F1** to get information about this window. In the middle of the Help window, you'll see the topic "Looking up the alignment values for your printer." Click on this topic to bring up the Help window shown in Figure 18.5 which lists many different models of page printers. Select the help topic for your printer (for example, HP LaserJet III). You'll then see information about which settings to enter in the Horiz and Vert fields in the Check Printer

Alignment window. (In many cases, Help will tell
you that no adjustment settings are necessary.)
6. Selct **OK** to confirm the alignment settings and
return to the Print Checks window. Click on
Print. Quicken will print your checks using the
partial page in the envelope feeder first.

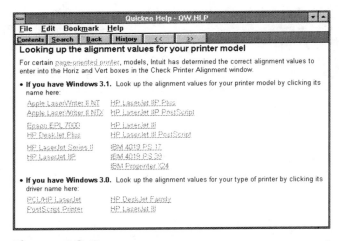

Figure 18.5 Help for adjusting page-oriented
printers

◆ *Lesson* ◆

19

Managing Memorized Transactions

Recalling a Memorized Transaction

As you know by now, Quicken "memorizes" everything about a transaction you enter except for the Date and Num field. The easiest way to recall a memorized transaction is to just start typing in the Payee field until Quicken "recalls" and retrieves the memorized transaction you want. In fact, the Payee drop-down list includes all transactions that have been memorized to date.

To practice this, let's create a new $150 ATM transaction assigned to the Misc category:

1. Press **Ctrl+N** to create a new transaction. Then type the date **8/18/92** in the Date field. Now press **Tab** to move to the Num field and then type **ATM** or choose it from the Num drop-down list. Press **Tab** to move to the Payee field.

2. Type **A** and Quicken fills in American Express, the first name in the Payee drop-down list in Figure 19.1 beginning with an A. Type **T**, how-

117

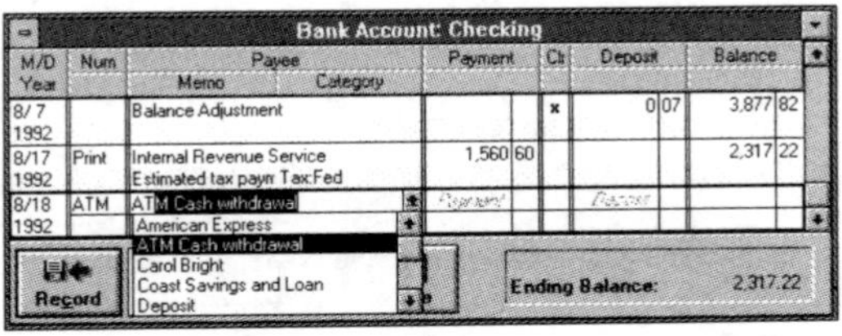

Figure 19.1 Recalling a memorized transaction

ever, and Quicken fills in ATM Cash withdrawal, just like in Figure 19.1.

3. Press **Tab** (don't click) to move to the Payment field, and Quicken fills in all the remaining fields of the memorized transaction, just like in Figure 19.2. In this case, the only additional field is the $200 Payment amount.

4. If you want, you can now change or add information. Here, for instance, type **150** to change the amount. Then press **Tab twice** to move to the Category field and type **Misc** or click on this choice in the Category drop-down list. Click on **Record** to save this transaction. You can see the completed transaction in Figure 19.3.

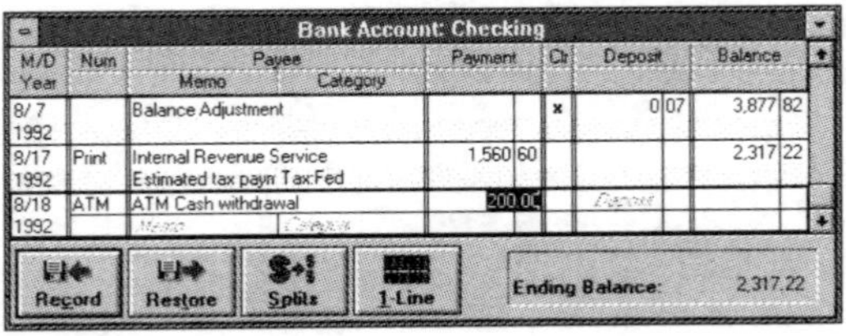

Figure 19.2 Changing part of a memorized transaction in the register

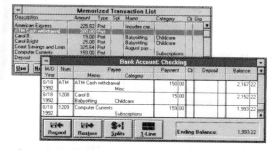

Figure 19.3   Viewing the Memorized
Transaction List

Viewing Memorized Transactions

Although the Payee drop-down list enables you to
choose memorized transactions, only the Memorized
Transaction List window provides the detail for each
memorized transaction. To open this window, press
Ctrl+T the shortcut for the Lists Memorized Transactions command. You'll access an alphabetized transactions list window like the one shown in Figure 19.3, in
which all memorized transactions for all accounts (except investments) reside.

Transactions Quicken Memorizes

The first time you enter a transaction it becomes a
memorized transaction. For instance, enter check 1209
to Computer Currents in Figure 19.3, and you can see
the resulting memorized transaction in the Memorized
Transaction List window.

Once a transaction has been memorized, a later
transaction using the same *exact* text in the Payee field

(case doesn't matter, however), does *not* update the
memorized transaction. For example, notice in the
Memorized Transaction List window that the $200
ATM cash withdrawal was not updated by the 8/18
$150 ATM withdrawal. (To update a memorized trans-
action, see "Editing a Memorized Transaction" in this
lesson.)

If a new transaction uses different text in the Payee
field, then Quicken memorizes that transaction without changing (updating) an existing memorized transaction. For example, enter check 1208 shown in Figure
19.3, where the last name Bright is abbreviated to B. in
the Payee field. You can see in the Memorized Transaction List that Quicken adds a new memorized transaction rather than changing the earlier memorized one
for Carol Bright.

Editing a Memorized Transaction

You can change a memorized transaction through the
Memorized Transaction List window. For example,
here's how to add a Misc category to the ATM memorized transaction in Figure 19.3 (or one of your own):

1. Open the Memorized Transaction List window by
   pressing **Ctrl+T** (shortcuts for the Lists Memorized Transactions command).
2. Click on the memorized transaction you want to
   change, in this case the $200 ATM Cash with-
   drawal. Then click on **Edit** at the bottom of the
   window to open the Edit Memorized Transaction
   dialog box shown in Figure 19.4.

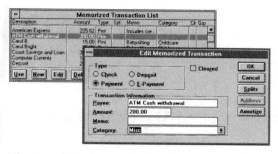

Figure 19.4   Editing a memorized transaction

3. Make the changes to the selected memorized transaction. In this example, click on the Category text box. Then type **Misc** or choose it from the Category drop-down list that appears. Click on **OK** to confirm your changes.

This change is now reflected in the Memorized Transaction List; if you now create a transaction in the register using this memorized transaction, it would include Misc in the Category field.

> **Tip**
> You can also use the Edit Memorized Transaction dialog box to create amortized loan payments. See Lesson 29.

Deleting a Memorized Transaction

After you've been entering transactions in Quicken for awhile, you should clean out the Memorized Transactions List. Use the Del button in this window to erase multiple entries for the same transaction—those with misspellings or slightly different wording in the Payee field. Deleting these entries is also an easy way to standardize how a particular transaction should appear.

Changing How Quicken Recalls Transactions

You can change how Quicken recalls memorized transactions by choosing the Edit Preferences QuickFill command to access the dialog box shown in Figure 19.5.

Two QuickFill settings control how Quicken recalls a memorized transaction. Both are on (checked) by default; to turn one or both off, click on the appropriate check boxes.

- **Automatic Completion as You Type an Entry** governs whether Quicken automatically completes an entry in a field when you type enough characters for it to recognize the entry. For example, this setting directs Quicken to add

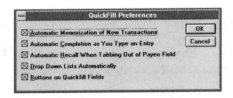

Figure 19.5   QuickFill settings govern the way Quicken memorizes and recalls transactions.

the highlighted text in the Payee field of Figure 19.1 when you type **AT**. This setting also controls Quicken's automatic completion when you begin to type in the Category field.

- **Automatic Recall When Tabbing Out of Payee Field** determines whether the rest of a memorized transaction is recalled when you press Tab to leave the Payee field. When you press Tab in Figure 19.1, for instance, this setting tells Quicken to add the rest of the memorized transaction shown in Figure 19.2.

Keep in mind, however, that when you turn off one or both of these settings, Quicken still memorizes transactions—you're just changing how memorized transactions are recalled. What's more, you can still recall a memorized transaction using the Memorized Transaction List window.

Two settings enable you to control the Payee and other drop-down lists:

- **Drop Down Lists Automatically** causes a drop-down list to open when you move to a field.
- **Buttons on QuickFill Fields** causes 🖩 to appear in a field so you can open a drop-down list.

Turning off Quicken's Automatic Memorization

The first QuickFill setting you see in Figure 19.5, Automatic memorization of new transactions, controls Quicken's automatic memorization. If you turn this setting off, thereafter, no transactions will be memorized.

When the Memorized Transaction List reaches 1,000 entries or so—about half of Quicken's 2,000 memorized transactions capability— Quicken turns off automatic memorization. (You'll see a message warning you when this happens.) If this occurs, you must clean out your Memorized Transaction List by deleting similar or unused entries, as explained earlier.

Manually Creating a Memorized Transaction

Even when Quicken's automatic memorization is turned off, you can still create memorized transactions. Simply enter a transaction and before you click on Record, memorize the transaction by pressing Ctrl+M, the shortcut for the Edit Memorize Transaction command. You'll see a dialog box saying "This transaction is about to be memorized." Click on OK to confirm, and Quicken beeps as it memorizes the transaction.

If the transaction has already been memorized, you'll see "Transaction already memorized" and three options: Replace to overwrite the memorized transaction, Add to insert a separate memorized transaction, and Cancel.

Printing a Memorized Transactions List

As long as the Memorized Transaction List window is open and active, you can print a paper copy of its contents by choosing the File Print List command. (If this window isn't open, you won't see Print List in the File menu.) When you see the Print Memorized Transaction List dialog box, accept the default of Printer and click on Print. (To change the default print settings Quicken uses, refer to Lesson 32.)

◆ *Lesson* ◆

20

Working with a Transaction Group

Setting Up a Transaction Group

Setting up a *transaction group* of one or more memo-rized transactions allows you to easily enter multiple recurring transactions, such as monthly bills—the mortgage, phone, electric, car payment, and so on. You can create up to 12 transaction groups.

There are two elements common to each transaction in a group:

- Each transaction occurs (or is paid) at the same time—monthly, quarterly, and so on.
- Each transaction occurs in the same register, such as a Checking register.

Tip
BillMinder can remind you when to pay the bills in a transaction group. (See Lesson 21.)

Let's set up a transaction group for two memorized transactions to be paid at the beginning of the month from the Checking register we've been working with:

1. Open the Transaction Group List window shown in Figure 20.1 by pressing **Ctrl+J**, the shortcut for the Lists Transaction Group command.
2. Open a transaction group by double-clicking on the first empty group, in this case **Group 1**. (Or click once on the group and then on Use). You'll see the Describe Group 1 dialog box shown in Figure 20.1.
3. Name the group and specify the group settings. In the first text box, name the group by typing **Regular**, or a descriptive name of your own 20 characters or less. Accept the default Type of transactions setting, **Regular**.
4. If you want, set up Reminder Settings for Billminder. (See Lesson 21.) Here, for instance, click on ⬛ to open the Frequency drop-down list, scroll down the list, and click on **Monthly**. Then click on the **Next scheduled date** text box; enter the

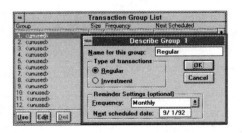

Figure 20.1   The Transaction Group List window

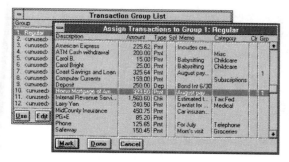

Figure 20.2   Assigning transactions to a group

next date you'll want to record or pay the grouped transactions. In this case, type **9/1/92**.

5. Click on **OK** to confirm these settings, and Quicken opens the Assign Transactions to Group 1: Regular window shown in Figure 20.2. This window contains the same memorized transactions as the Memorized Transactions List window.

6. Mark each memorized transaction you want in the Regular group by double-clicking on the transaction. (Or click on the transaction and then click on Mark.) In this case, double-click on the **Home Mortgage** memorized transaction and then the **Coast Savings and Loan** transaction. Notice that Quicken adds the number of the group (1 in this case) to each in the Grp column.

7. When you finish assigning memorized transactions to the group, click on **Done**. You'll be returned to the Transaction Group List window shown at the back of Figure 20.3, where you can

Figure 20.3   Using a Transaction Group

see that Group 1 is named Regular and includes two memorized transactions. (The Use Transaction Group dialog box will be employed next to execute this group.)

To delete a selected transaction group, select it and then click on Del in the Transaction Group List window. When you're asked to confirm the deletion, click on OK. This deletes just the group, not the memorized transactions assigned to that group.

Executing a Transaction Group

Once you create a transaction group, you can execute it—tell Quicken to enter the group in the register. Here's how to execute the Regular group or a transaction group of your own:

1. If the Transaction Group List window isn't open, open it by pressing **Ctrl+J**, the shortcut for the Lists Transaction Group command.
2. Select the group you want to execute. In this case double-click on **Regular**. You'll see the Use

Transaction Group dialog box shown in Figure 20.3.

3. Specify where you want the transactions posted. In this case, accept the Target account, **Checking**. (To access a different account, click on ▣ to open the Target account drop-down list and click on the one you want.) Likewise, accept the Transaction date, 9/1/92, or type a different one in this text box. (If you don't include a date, Quicken will use the current date when you execute the transaction group.)

4. Click on **OK** to confirm these settings Quicken beeps as it opens the Checking register shown in Figure 20.4 and enters each of the grouped transactions in the Regular group, all dated 9/1/92. When you see the message indicating this is complete, click on **OK**. The Checking register remains the active window.

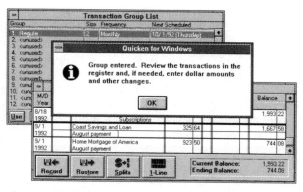

Figure 20.4 Posting grouped transactions to the register

5. Make any changes you want to the posted transactions. In Figure 20.4, for practice, click on the **Num** field of the Coast Savings and Loan transaction and then type **1210**. Click on the **Memo field** and press **Del** until the memo is erased, click on the **Category field** and type **Auto:Loan**, then click on **Record** to save these changes. Make the same changes to the Home Mortgage of America transaction, except specify check **1211** and a **Housing** category.

6. Close the Transaction Group List window (it's still open behind the register) by pressing **Ctrl+F6** to first make it the active window; then double-click on its window control box ▣ .

Changing a Transaction Group

You can change a transaction group by assigning additional memorized transactions or by removing some. Using an approach similar to setting up a transaction group, you click on the group you want to change in the Transaction Group List window, such as Regular, then click on Edit to return to the Assign Transactions to Group 1: Regular window in Figure 20.3. In this window you can ungroup a memorized transaction already assigned to Grp 1 by double-clicking on it or mark other transactions to add them to the group. When you've made the changes, click on Done.

21

Billminder

What is Billminder?

Billminder is a separate utility program that is copied to your disk automatically when you install Quicken, even if you elect not to run it. When you start Windows (or your PC), Billminder reminds you that post-dated checks need printing, transaction groups contain bills that need to be paid, or electronic payments need to be transmitted.

In addition to Billminder, Quicken also has a built-in Reminder window, which appears when you start Quicken for all the same reasons as Billminder. But don't confuse Billminder with the Reminder window; they are two entirely different entities and appear at different times. The Reminder window appears when you start Quicken. Billminder appears when you start Windows (or if so configured, whenever you start your PC); it is designed as a reminder *to use Quicken*.

Controlling Billminder

In Lesson 1, we recommended that you accept the default setting that turns Billminder on during Quicken's installation. Here's how to change this and other Billminder settings:

1. Select the **Preferences Billminder** command to access the dialog box in Figure 21.1.
2. If it isn't already on, activate Billminder by clicking on the **Turn on Billminder** check box.
3. If you want, click on the text box and type how many days in advance you want to be reminded; 3 is the default and is usually sufficient.
4. Click on **OK** to confirm your settings.

To understand how Billminder behaves, refer to the check to the IRS written on 8/17/92 in Lesson 16. If you didn't print the check in Lesson 17 and Billminder is set to remind you three days in advance, then from 8/14/92 to 8/17/92 you'd see the Billminder icon (a hand with a string tied around the forefinger) at the foot of the screen whenever you start Windows. Click on this icon and you'd see the reminder, "You have checks to print." If you still haven't printed the check after 8/17/92, you'd see an overdue checks reminder.

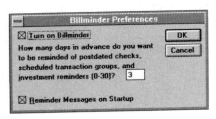

Figure 21.1 Setting up Billminder

◆ *Lesson* ◆

22

Working with Categories

Setting Up Your Own Categories

In Quicken, categories enable you to allocate income and expenses. By managing this allocation, you can use categories to:

- Track income tax deductions
- Summarize cash flow—inflows (deposits) and outflows (payments)
- Create a budget

You'll want to establish categories that reflect your income and spending habits—for example, two salaries, interest for two car loans, commuting expense, and the like. Keep in mind, however, that it can be easier to use categories designed for taxes and then create subcategories for your particular income and expenses. (You'll work with subcategories in Lesson 23.)

Tip
To allocate a mortgage payment to interest and principal, see Lesson 29.

Setting Up Categories for Tax Purposes

Because many of Quicken's existing categories correspond to subtotals and some line items on federal tax forms, you shouldn't have to create many new categories for tax purposes. For instance, **Int Inc** corresponds to Line 4 on Schedule B (Line 8a on Form 1040). The subcategory **Taxes:Real Est** corresponds to real estate taxes entered as a line item (line 6) on Schedule A.

In fact, you can see the Federal form to which a category is assigned if you:

1. Choose the **Preferences General** command to access the dialog box shown in Figure 22.1.
2. Turn on the **Use Tax Schedules with Categories** option by clicking on its check box.
3. Click on **OK** to confirm this setting.

Now when you access the Category & Transfer List window and edit a category, you'll see the tax form to

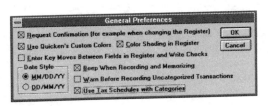

Figure 22.1 Displaying federal forms for categories

which a category is linked. What's more, when you create a new category, you'll be able to assign it to a tax form, which makes it easy later to print reports specifically for tax purposes (Lesson 31).

The easiest way to set up categories for taxes is to grab last year's tax book or forms. Create categories for lines that sum items; create subcategories for the line items making up each subtotal. For instance, you might want to use Quicken's category for interest income reported on Schedule B, but then create subcategories for each source of interest income. You'll see how to do this in Lesson 23.

Creating a Category

Suppose you perform some consulting, and need a category to keep track of this income. Here's how to add this category to the Category list, or to create a category of your own choosing:

1. Open the Category & Transfer List window by clicking on ![icon] in the IconBar or pressing **Ctrl+C**, both shortcuts for the Lists Category & Transfer command. Quicken opens a Category List window like the one shown in Figure 22.2 and makes it the active window.
2. Click on **New** at the bottom of the window to access the Set Up Category dialog box shown in Figure 22.2.
3. Name and describe the category. In the Name text box, enter a name 14 characters or less. In this case, type **Consulting Inc**. If you want, click on the Description text box and enter a description up to 24 characters.

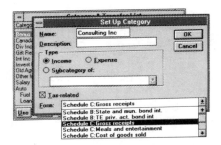

Figure 22.2 Adding a category

4. Specify the type of category. In this case, change the default of Expense by clicking on the **Income** radio button.

5. If appropriate, as in this case, click on the **Tax-related** check box to designate this category for tax purposes. Then click on ▪ to open the Form drop-down list shown. Scroll down this list and click on **Schedule C:Gross receipts**. (If you don't see the Form text box, see "Setting Up Categories for Tax Purposes," above.)

6. Click on **OK** to confirm these settings and return to the Category & Transfer List window. You can see in Figure 22.3 how Quicken adds this new category to the alphabetized list.

7. If you want, close the Category List window by double-clicking on its window control box ▫.

Tip

When you enter a nonexisting category for a check or transaction and click on Record, you'll see a dialog box saying that Quicken couldn't find the category. To add this category, click on

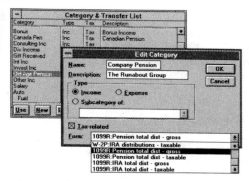

Figure 22.3 Editing a category

Set Up to access the Set Up Category dialog box shown in Figure 22.2. Specify the settings you want; when you click on OK, Quicken adds the category to the Category & Transfer List.

Changing a Category

By editing a category, you can personalize an existing category. Changing a category is also an efficient way to enter a category of your own and simultaneously eliminate an existing category you won't ever use. In fact, when you change a category that has already been assigned to transactions or checks, Quicken automatically updates their Category fields.

Suppose, for instance, you receive a company pension, but bristle a little at the wording, "Old Age Pension." Here's how to change this category or one you choose:

1. With the Category & Transfer List window open (click on in the IconBar if it isn't), click on the category you want to change, **Old Age Pension** in this case, so that it's highlighted.

2. Click on **Edit** at the bottom of the window to access an Edit Category dialog box like the one shown in Figure 22.3. This dialog box will reflect all the current settings of the Old Age Pension category.

⇨ **Note:** Because the Form text box is blank, you know that this category currently won't be printed on any tax reports you generate.

3. Change the appropriate settings. For example, type **Company Pension** in the Name text box. Then press **Tab** and type the company name, **The Runabout Group**, in the Description text box. Accept the other existing settings—**Type of Income** and **Tax-related** turned on.

4. If you want to designate this category as a Federal line item, click on ⬲ to open the Form drop-down list. Then use the scroll bar to move to the end of the list and click on **1099R:Pension total dist-gross**.

Category	Type	Tax	Description
Bonus	Inc	Tax	Bonus Income
Canada Pen	Inc	Tax	Canadian Pension
Company Pension	Inc	Tax	The Runabout Group
Consulting Inc	Inc	Tax	
Div Income	Inc	Tax	Dividend Income
Gift Received	Inc	Tax	Gift Received
Int Inc	Inc	Tax	Interest Income
Invest Inc	Inc	Tax	Investment Income
Other Inc	Inc	Tax	Other Income
Salary	Inc	Tax	Salary Income
Auto	Expns		Automobile Expenses
Fuel	Sub		Auto Fuel

Category & Transfer List

`Use` `New` `Edit` `Del`

Figure 22.4 Changing a category

Tip

If you can't find a Federal line item in the Form list, such as Total pensions and annuities on Line 17 of Form 1040, there's usually a listing for the form on which the item is reported to you, such as 1099R in this case.

5. Click on **OK** to confirm these settings and return to the Category & Transfer List window. You can see in Figure 22.4 how Quicken moves this edited category to its respective place in the alphabetized list.

Deleting a Category

To delete a category, such as Canada Pen in Figure 22.4, simply click on it and then click on Del the bottom of the Category & Transfer List window. You'll see a dialog box asking you to confirm that the category should be deleted by clicking on OK. Be aware, however, that Quicken also deletes all references to the deleted category in any checks and transactions.

Printing a Category List

To print a listing of categories (and subcategories):

1. Make sure that the Category & Transfer List window is active.
2. Press **Ctrl+P**, the shortcut for the File Print List command. In the dialog box that appears, accept the Print to default of **Printer** and click on **Print**.

23

Working with Subcategories

What is a Subcategory?

A *subcategory* is a subheading under a category. In Figure 23.1, for instance, Fuel, Loan, and Service are all subcategories of the Auto category. When you generate a report and subcategories are present, Quicken lists the subcategory amounts and creates a category total. In this way, Fuel, Loan, and Service expenses would be listed and totalled under the Auto category. You may assign up to 15 subcategories to a particular category.

Adding a Subcategory

Suppose you want to track your and your spouse's salaries separately, but want them totalled on any reports you create for income tax and budget purposes. Here's how to set up Salary subcategories to do this. You can also use this approach to set up other subcategories of your own:

1. With the Category & Transfer List window open (click on ⬛ in the IconBar or press **Ctrl+C** if it

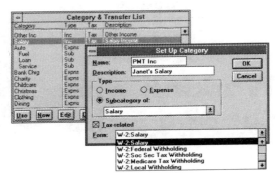

Figure 23.1   Creating a subcategory

isn't), click on **New** at the bottom of the window to access the Set Up Category dialog box shown in Figure 23.1.

2. Name and describe the Subcategory. In the Name text box, enter a subcategory name 14 characters or less. In Figure 23.1, for instance, type **PMT Inc**. If you want, click on the Description text box and type a description no more than 24 characters, such as **Janet's Salary**.

3. Specify to which category you want the subcategory attached. Click on the **Subcategory of:** radio button. In the Subcategory text box, type the category name, **Salary** in this example. Or click on to open the drop-down list, go to Salary by scrolling to it or typing **s**, and then click on this choice.

4. If appropriate, as in this case, click on the **Tax-related** check box to designate this category for tax purposes. Then click on to open the Form drop-down list and use the scroll bar to scroll

down this list. Click on **W-2: Salary**. (If you don't see the Form text box, refer back to Lesson 22.)

➡️ **Note:** Even if a category is already assigned to a Federal line item, you must assign each subcategory to the line item as well or to one of the forms that feed that line item. For instance, W-2 forms are used to create the total for Line 7 on Form 1040, called "Wages, salaries, tips, etc." Otherwise, the subcategory and its corresponding amount won't appear on any tax reports you create.

5. Click on **OK** to confirm these settings and return to the Category & Transfer List window. You can see in Figure 23.2 how Quicken adds the PMT Inc subcategory to the Salary category.

6. If you want, for practice, repeat this technique and add the **County Medical** subcategory shown and assign it to **W-2:Salary** in the Form drop-down list.

Figure 23.2 After adding a subcategory

After you add one or more subcategories to a category, you should go back and reassign any transactions using that category. For example, you'd now want to search through the register (see Lesson 10) for any transactions with Salary in the Category field and reassign them to one of the subcategories. Otherwise, when you print reports, the transactions assigned to Salary appear under Salary:Other. (Remember, subcategories are totalled at the category level.)

Managing Subcategories

Subcategories are changed or deleted in the same way as categories. (See Lesson 22.) When you delete a subcategory, however, Quicken automatically assigns the transactions and checks that were in the subcategory to its category. If you delete the Salary subcategories in Figure 23.2, for instance, any transactions and checks referring to these subcategories would be adjusted to refer to the Salary category.

 ### Tip

If a subcategory becomes a significant expense or source of income, you can promote it to a category. In the Category & Transfer List window, click on the subcategory and then click on Edit to access the Edit Category dialog box. Then change the Type from Subcategory to Income or Expense.

◆ *Lesson* ◆

24
Working with Split Transactions

What is a Split Transaction?

A *split transaction* is a check or transaction allocated to one or more of these:

- Categories or subcategories
- Accounts, such as a liability account for a mortgage

For instance, you can split an ATM withdrawal between gas, entertainment, and miscellaneous categories, or allocate your paycheck to taxes and income. And, if you set up a liability account for a mortgage, you can split a mortgage payment between mortgage interest and principal repayment of this liability. (Lesson 27 shows how to split a mortgage payment.)

Splitting an Existing Transaction or Check

Suppose you decide to allocate the $150 ATM withdrawal shown in Figure 24.1 to gas, entertainment, and

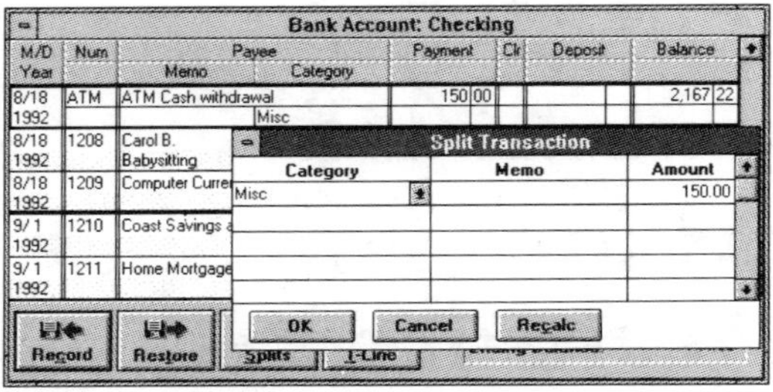

Figure 24.1   Splitting a transaction

food. To split this transaction or to split one of your
own transactions or checks:

1. Select the transaction to split, the $150 ATM
   withdrawal, by clicking on any of its fields.
2. Click on **Splits** at the bottom of the register to
   open the Split Transaction dialog box shown in
   Figure 24.1.. Notice how Quicken copies the
   150.00 payment amount and any existing category information—Misc in this case—to the first
   line of the split.
3. Split the transaction. In the first line, type the
   category or subcategory (and a class, if appropriate) to which you want to allocate part of the
   transaction, such as **Auto:Fuel** as in Figure 24.2.
   If you want, press **Tab** and enter a memo in the
   Memo field. In this case, press **Tab twice** to
   move to the Amount field and type the gas
   amount, **30**. When you press **Tab** to move to the
   second line, Quicken subtracts this amount from
   the $150 transaction amount and shows the dif-
   ference—120.00—on the next line.

			Bank Account: Checking					
M/D Year	Num	Payee		Payment	Ck	Deposit	Balance	▲
		Memo	Category					
8/18 1992	ATM	ATM Cash withdrawal		150 00			2,167 22	
8/18 1992	1208		--Splits--				2,152 22	

Split Transaction

Category	Memo	Amount	▲
Auto:Fuel		30.00	
Entertain	Amusement park	50.00	
Groceries		70.00	

1,993.22
744.08

[OK]   [Cancel]   [Recalc]

Figure 24.2 Allocating part of the transaction to a subcategory

Tip

If you're not sure of the categories to use, click on at any time to open the Category & Transfer List window. When you double-click on a category from the list, Quicken adds it to the current Category field in the Split Transaction dialog box.

4. Allocate the remaining amount, $120 in this case, to the different categories. Type **En** so that Quicken completes Entertain. Press **Tab** and type **Amusement park** in the Memo field; press **Tab** again and type **50**. Press **Tab** to move to the third line and type **Gro** so that Quicken completes Groceries for you. Because Quicken maintains a running difference, you don't have to enter 70.00. Your dialog box should now look like Figure 24.2.

5. Assign these categories to the transaction by clicking on **OK**. Quicken returns you to the trans-

action in the register window shown in Figure 24.2. Notice that --Splits-- appears in the Category field indicating that the transaction is assigned to multiple categories.

6. Click on **Record** to record the split transaction.

Tip

If the existing amount of a transaction or check is incorrect, you can change it in the Split Transaction dialog box. Enter the correct amounts for each of the categories. Then click on Recalc before you click on OK. This tells Quicken to first sum the entries and then replace the old payment or deposit amount in the transaction with this new total.

Splitting a Paycheck

Splitting a paycheck works a little differently because the cash transaction represents net salary, not gross salary. Gross salary needs to be allocated to income; the difference between gross and net represents taxes withheld by your employer, which must be allocated as expenses.

With this in mind, we'll use a $1,545.36 paycheck deposit ($2,000 gross) to demonstrate the procedure for this.

1. Click on the **Category** field of the deposit and then click on **Splits** to open the Split Transaction dialog box. The 1,545.36 deposit amount and the existing Salary category appear on the first line of the split.

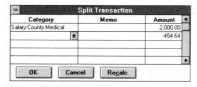

Figure 24.3 Allocating gross
salary to a category

2. Allocate the gross salary to the Salary subcategory County Medical created in Lesson 23 by pressing **End** to move to the end of this category and then typing **:**. Quicken fills in County Medical for you. Now press **Tab twice** and type the **2000** gross salary in the Amount field. When you press **Tab** to move to the second line, Figure 24.3 shows how Quicken calculates a negative difference of –454.64, which represents the amount of taxes withheld (2,000–1,545.36). (Don't worry that taxes are allocated as negative amounts here— Quicken is just making the distinction between income and expenses.)

3. Allocate the negative difference to **Tax** subcategories. (You should be able to get these amounts from your pay stub.) For example, assign the tax subcategories and amounts shown in Figure 24.4 by typing **Tax:** so that Quicken adds the Fed subcategory; press **Tab** twice or click on the **Amount** field and then type **–250**. Press **Tab** to move to the third line, click on ⊠ to open the Category list, type **Tax:** and then click on **Tax:Soc Sec**. click on the **Amount** field in this line and then type **-150.2**. Press **Tab** to move to the fourth line, open the Category list

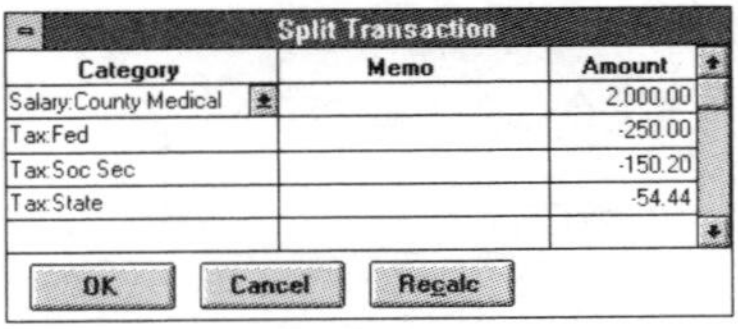

Category	Memo	Amount
Salary:County Medical		2,000.00
Tax:Fed		-250.00
Tax:Soc Sec		-150.20
Tax:State		-54.44

OK   Cancel   Re*g*alc

Figure 24.4   Allocating to Tax subcategories

and choose **Tax:State**. Since Quicken maintains a running difference, -54.44 is already entered for you.

4. Save this allocation by clicking on **OK** in the Split Transaction dialog box. --Splits-- now appears in the Category field of the deposit transaction.

5. Click on **Record** in the register window to save the split transaction.

Splitting a New Transaction or Check

With one exception, splitting a new transaction or check works the same as splitting an existing one. If you haven't yet entered the amount in the Payment or Deposit field, then Quicken takes the amount from the total in the Split Transaction dialog box. A positive total is entered in the Deposit field; a negative total is entered as a positive amount in the Payment field. Make sure, then, that you enter all amounts representing a payment as negative in the Split Transaction dialog box.

Deleting All or Part of a Split Transaction

In the Split Transaction dialog box, you can delete the current line (and thus the entry in the line) by pressing Ctrl+D. Quicken then automatically recalculates the new difference.

However, Quicken won't let you select a Category field containing --Splits--; therefore, the only way to delete a split Category field is to use Ctrl+D repeatedly in the Split Transaction dialog box to delete every filled line. When you click on OK, Quicken deletes --Splits-- in the Category field of the transaction or check.

◆ *Lesson* ◆

25

Working with Multiple Accounts

Types of Quicken Accounts

An account is composed of related transactions, such as the deposits and payments that occur in a checking account. Checking, savings, and money market accounts are essentially the same animal—a bank account in which you enter deposits and withdraw funds. Naturally, if you have separate checking and savings accounts, you'll want to create additional Quicken accounts to track each one individually. Other Quicken account types shown in Table 25.1 enable you to track different types of financial data. As examples, you can establish a liability account to track a home mortgage and an asset account to track the basis (value) of your home.

Only by adding your accounts to Quicken (do it slowly over time!) can you generate a true financial picture for yourself. For example, you'll be able to track your home basis and mortgage; or, once all assets and liabilities are included in Quicken, to calculate your net worth.

Table 25.1   Types of Quicken Accounts

Quicken Type	Use for
Bank Account	Checking and savings accounts, money market accounts
Cash Account	Petty cash account—usually used in a business
Credit Card	Credit card accounts
Asset	Home basis, rental property, loans you've made, other assets such as a boat
Other Liability	Mortgage, car loans, student loans, bank loans, credit lines
Investment	Stocks, bonds, and mutual funds

Viewing an Account List

You can view the accounts you've created in Quicken by clicking on ▦ in the IconBar or pressing Ctrl+A. Both are shortcuts for the Lists Account command. You'll see an Account List window like the one in Figure 25.1. If you haven't created any accounts since starting Quicken for the first time, you'll just see your Checking account. (To close this window, double-click on its window control box ▣.)

Notice that the Account List provides up-to-the-minute information about each account. In Figure 25.1, for instance, you can see that the Checking account contains 25 transactions and a current balance of 744.08.

Figure 25.1 An Account List window

And because ✔ appears in the Chks column, you know that Checking contains checks written in the Write Checks window.

Adding a New Account

Suppose you want to open an account for savings, which contains $10,000 on 8/1/92. To do this:

1. Select the **Activities Create New Account** command. You'll see the dialog box shown in Figure 25.2. Since a savings account is a bank account, click on **OK** to accept this account type and access the dialog box in Figure 25.3. (This dialog box is identical to the one you saw in Lesson 2.)

2. In the Account Name text box, type **Savings** or a name up to 15 characters. Then press **Tab** or click on the **Balance** text box. Type the beginning balance of this new account, **10000** in this case. Press **Tab** to move to the date text box and enter the date of this balance, **8/1/92**. If you want, click in the **Description** text box and type a description 21 characters or less, such as **Coast 334687**.

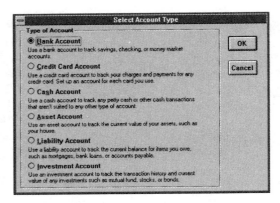

Figure 25.2   Specifying the account type

Tip
When figuring the beginning balance, don't forget any uncleared deposits or withdrawals open on the starting date.

3. Click on **OK** to confirm these settings and Quicken opens the Savings account register in Figure 25.4 containing one transaction—the $10,000 opening balance.

Figure 25.3   Opening a savings account

Note: Although you can use the New button in the Account List window to create a new account, you'll then have to double-click on the account (or highlight the account and then click on the Use button in this window) to open its register.

Opening Multiple Account Registers

Since each register is a window, you can use the Account List window to open multiple accounts. In fact, Quicken lets you keep as many as eight accounts open at any one time.

For example, with the Savings account register in Figure 25.4 open, you can open the Checking account by first clicking on [ACCT] in the IconBar to open the Account List window. Then double-click anywhere on the Checking account line (or highlight the account and then click on Use). This opens the Checking register and makes it the active window.

M/D Year	Num	Payee / Memo Category	Payment	Cl	Deposit	Balance	
8/1 1992		Opening Balance [Savings]		x	10,000 00	10,000 00	
8/21 1992	*Num*	*Payee* / *Memo* *Category*	*Payment*		*Deposit*		

Bank Account: Savings

| Record | Restore | Splits | 1-Line | Ending Balance: | 10,000.00 |

Figure 25.4 The register for the new Savings account

Tip
The Activities Use Register command and its shortcuts ▦ and Ctrl+R open the last account register that was open and active in Quicken. You can also customize the 💲 icon in the IconBar to open a specific account.

Changing a Beginning Balance

In a register window, you can change any of the settings you specified for a new account, such as the date or beginning balance. Just click on the Opening Balance transaction, make the changes, and then click on Record to record the changes.

You can also change the account name and description through the Account List window. For instance, when you click on Savings and then on Edit at the bottom of the window, the Edit Account Information dialog box appears. Simply click on OK, and any changes you make are immediately reflected in the Account List window and in the title bar of the register window.

Deleting an Account

Although you can delete an existing account through the Account List window, you'll rarely want to do this. Deleting an account erases it from Quicken and *all* of the transactions in that account.

In fact, Quicken makes you perform an extra confirmation step when you try to delete an account. If, for instance, you click on an account, such as our sample Savings account, and then on Del at the bottom of the Account List window, Quicken displays the Delete Account dialog box, in which you must *type* (not just click) **Yes** in the text box before clicking on OK.

26

Working with Transfer Transactions

What is a Transfer Transaction?

A *transfer transaction* occurs between two accounts. For example, transferring $500 from a savings account to a checking account is a transfer transaction you're no doubt familiar with. In this case, the transfer reallocates cash between two bank (asset) accounts—checking and savings; the savings balance decreases while the checking balance increases by the same amount.

In Quicken, transfer transactions are also used to allocate transactions to asset or liability accounts. For example, you'll learn in Lesson 30 how to use a transfer transaction to allocate part of a mortgage payment to principal.

Since a transfer transaction affects two accounts, Quicken provides an easy way to create both sides of the transaction. You use the bracketed account references listed at the end of the Category & Transfer List window, like those shown in Figure 26.1, to create the transfer. (These accounts also appear at the bottom of the Category drop-down list.) It's important to under-

Figure 26.1 Using account listings to create a transfer

stand that you'll be using the Category & Transfer List just as a means to create the second side of the transfer transaction; you are *not* allocating an income or expense.

Tip
Although you can't assign a category to a transfer transaction, you can track a transfer by adding a class.

Creating a Transfer Transaction

To see how a transfer transaction works, let's transfer $2,000 on 9/1/92 between the Savings account created in Lesson 25 and the Checking account.

1. In one of the accounts, create the transfer transaction. In the Savings register window shown in Figure 26.2, for instance, create the transfer from savings to checking by first pressing **Ctrl+N** to create a new blank transaction.

 Note: You don't need to have both registers open, as in Figure 26.2. Both are open here so that you can see what the accounts look like before and after.

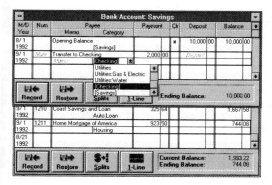

Figure 26.2   Creating a transfer transaction

2. Enter the transfer transaction. In this case, type **8/20/92** in the Date field, press **Tab**, and then type **Transfer to Checking** in the Payee field. Press **Tab** again and type **2000** in the Payment field. Move to the Category field by clicking on this text box.

3. In the Category field, specify the account to which the money will be transferred. In this example, type **[** and Quicken completes **[Checking]**, the first account listed in the Category & Transfer List shown in Figure 26.1 and the category drop-down list. (Pressing **+**, will cycle through the account listings.)

4. Click on **Record** to save this transfer transaction.

You can see in Figure 26.3 that Quicken not only records this transaction—a withdrawal—in the Savings register window, but also enters the corresponding transaction—a deposit—in the Checking register window.

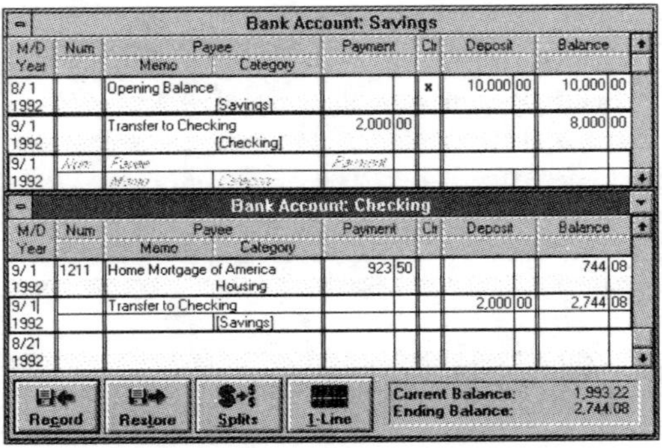

Figure 26.3 After entering a transfer transaction

It doesn't matter in which account you enter the transfer transaction. If you had entered the transfer transaction in this example as a 2,000 deposit in the Checking register, Quicken would have created the corresponding payment (withdrawal) transaction in the Savings register.

⇨ **Note:** If, after you create a transfer transaction, you decide to change a portion of it, be aware that the change will be reflected only in the Category field, the date, or the amount (Payment or Deposit field) in the other half of the transfer.

Deleting or Voiding a Transfer Transaction

When you delete a transfer transaction in one register, the corresponding transaction in the second register is also deleted. Voiding a transfer transaction works much the same way—the other half of the transaction is also voided—but only the 0 amount appears in both registers. The cleared symbol X and *VOID* in front of the description appear only in the transaction in which the void took place.

Going To the Other Side of a Transfer Transaction

When a transfer transaction is selected, the Edit Go To Transfer command provides a quick way to move to the corresponding transaction in the second account. To see how this works, try these steps:

1. With the Checking account register shown in Figure 26.3 open, click on the **$2,000** transfer transaction on 9/1/92.
2. Press **Ctrl+X**, the shortcut for the Edit Go To Transfer command. (If a transfer transaction isn't selected, you'll see the message "This item is not a transfer.")

If necessary, Quicken opens the account register containing the other half of the transaction—the Savings register in this case. Then it automatically moves to the corresponding transfer transaction in the Savings register.

◆ *Lesson* ◆

27

Working with Credit Card Accounts

Creating a Credit Card Account

In Quicken, you can create special Credit Card accounts that allow you to:

- Track credit card charges and advances
- Reconcile a credit card account
- Pay the bill

Suppose you have a MasterCard with a $5,000 limit, and the ending balance on your 8/1/92 statement is $1,561.80. Like other accounts, you can use the Activities Create New Account command (see Lesson 25) to open a credit card account such as MasterCard shown in Figure 27.1. There are, however, two special features:

- The Credit Limit text box allows you to enter a credit card limit, such as $5,000.
- The IntelliCharge check box, when you have an IntelliCharge account, lets you pull in credit card transactions (by modem or floppy) and pay the bill electronically.

Figure 27.1 Creating a Credit
Card account

The Credit Card Register

When you open a Credit Card register window, like the
one shown in Figure 27.2, you'll immediately realize
that the account terminology is designed specifically
for credit cards. To see how a credit card register works,
try entering the transactions shown.

First, notice that anything you charge, such as 35.50
at Carpo's on 8/5/92, is entered in the Charge field and
increases the outstanding balance. Any credit, such as
a return, would be entered in the Payment field and
would decrease the outstanding balance. By assigning a

M/D Year	Ref	Payee / Memo / Category	Charge		Clr	Payment		Balance	
8/1 1992		Opening Balance [MasterCard]	1,561	80	x			1,561	80
8/5 1992		Carpo's Entertain	35	50				1,537	30
8/15 1992		Macy's Clothing	65	20				1,662	50
8/20 1992		Mastercard [Checking]				500	00	1,162	50
8/25 1992	101	Cash Advance [Checking]	300	00				1,462	50
8/31 1992	Ref	Payee Memo Category	Charge			Payment			

Credit Card: MasterCard

Record	Restore	Splits	1-Line

Credit Remaining: 3,537.50
Ending Balance: 1,462.50

Figure 27.2 Credit Card register window

category such as Entertain (or even a split transaction), you can allocate a charge to an expense, in the same way that you allocate a check in a bank account.

Second, notice that any cash that flows into or out of a credit card account is represented by a transfer transaction. For instance, the $500 payment on 8/20/92 occurs in the Checking account. Likewise, the $300 advance drawn on MasterCard on 8/25/92 is deposited in Checking through a transfer transaction, although this may not always be the case.

28

Reconciling a Credit Card Account

The Credit Card Reconciliation Process

Quicken provides a way to reconcile a credit card account that works much the same as reconciling a bank account covered in Lessons 12 through 15. For instance, suppose the 9/1/92 statement for the MasterCard account created in Lesson 27 (Figure 27.2) shows new charges and cash advances of $400.70, a $500 payment, $40 in finance charges, and an ending balance of $1,502.50. The following sections will show you how to reconcile this MasterCard account or a credit card account of your own.

Entering Statement Information

In Quicken, the first step in the reconciliation process is to enter summary information from the credit card statement. Here's how to enter the 9/1/92 MasterCard

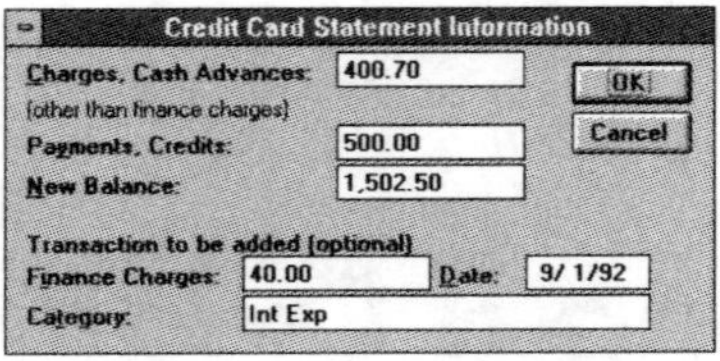

Figure 28.1 Beginning a credit card reconciliation

statement information (or information from your own statement):

1. With the MasterCard register open and active, click on ⚖ in the IconBar, the shortcut for the Activities Pay Credit Card Bill command. You'll see the dialog box shown in Figure 28.1.

2. Enter the total charges, payments, and credits during the statement period. In the Charges, Cash Advances text box, type the total new charges and advances, **400.70** in this case. Then click on the **Payments, Credits** text box and type the total payments and credits in the statement without a dollar sign. In this example, type **500**.

3. Click on the **New Balance** text box and type the ending balance shown on the credit card statement, **1,502.50**.

4. If you have *not* entered any finance charges as a transaction in the credit card register, click on the **Finance Charges** text box and type the amount, **40** in this case. Next, press **Tab** to move to the date text box and type the date the service charge occurred, **9/1/92**.

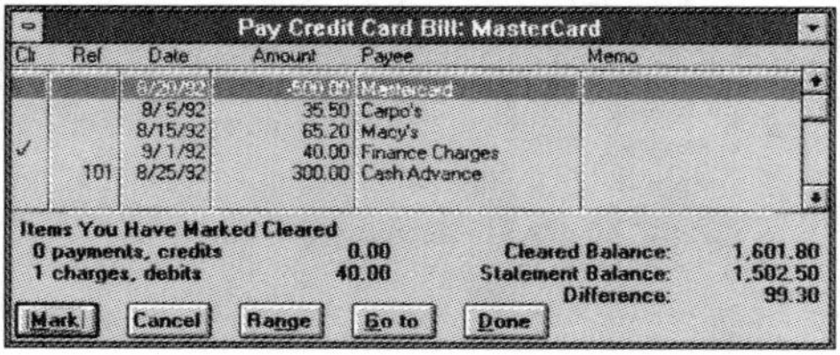

Figure 28.2   The Reconcile window

To assign a category, click on the **Category** text box and type **Int Exp**. (Or open the Category List window and choose one there.) Quicken automatically enters a cleared finance charge transaction even though you haven't confirmed these settings yet.

5. Click on **OK** to confirm this information and continue the reconciliation process. You'll now see the Reconcile window shown in Figure 28.2.

Working in the Credit Card Reconcile Window

As when you reconcile a bank account, the Reconcile window initially lists all transactions *not* currently cleared in the credit card account, such as the MasterCard register. You use the Reconcile window to mark transactions as cleared and to keep track of the amount by which the reconciled account balance and the ending credit card statement balance do not reconcile.

In this exercise, let's assume that each uncleared item appears in the MasterCard statement. Figure 28.3

Figure 28.3   A reconciled credit card account

shows how the Reconcile window appears after you
double-click on each item to mark it as cleared (✔).
Since the Difference at the bottom of the window is 0,
the MasterCard account and the credit card statement
are reconciled. (Lesson 15 discusses how to mark transactions and what to do if a transaction is incorrect or
missing. Lesson 16 discusses what to look for when the
Difference isn't 0.)

Completing the Reconciliation

Once you've completed the reconciliation, simply click
on Done to tell Quicken you're finished. If the Difference is $0.00, you'll see the dialog box shown in Figure
28.4.

⇒ **Note:** If the Difference isn't 0, you'll see an
Adjusting Register to Agree with Statement dialog
box. From here, you can tell Quicken to make an
adjusting transaction in the credit card register
equalling the Difference amount. (Refer back to
Lesson 14 before you do this.)

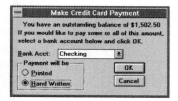

Figure 28.4 Paying the bill

You now have the option of letting Quicken enter the transaction or write the check to pay the bill. If you don't want Quicken to pay the bill, click on Cancel.

Paying the Bill

In the Make Credit Card payment dialog box shown in Figure 28.4, you can let Quicken enter the transfer transaction to pay the credit card bill. Don't worry that the amount will be equal to the current credit card balance—you'll be able to change it. For instance, here's how to pay $400 of this MasterCard bill:

1. Specify the bank account from which the bill should be paid. In this case, click on and then **checking** in the drop-down list that appears.
2. Specify who will write the check, you or Quicken. In this case, click on the **Hand Written** radio button.
3. Click on **OK** to confirm these settings. Figure 28.5 shows how Quicken opens the Checking register window and enters a transfer transaction to the MasterCard account for the entire credit card balance. Quicken hasn't recorded this trans-

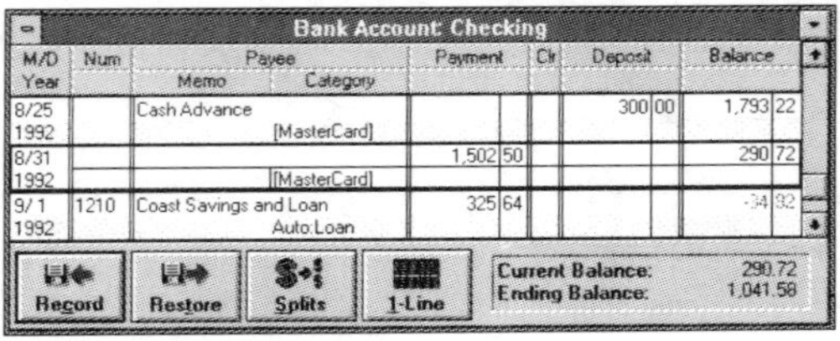

Figure 28.5 The transaction Quicken initially enters to pay the credit card bill

action yet—it is waiting for you to enter the amount you want to pay. (If you clicked on the Printed radio button, you'd see this transaction as a check in the Write Checks window.)

4. In the transfer transaction, click on the **Payee** field and type **MasterCard**, click on the **Payment** field and type the amount you want to pay, **400**. If you want, also click on the **Num** field and type the check number, **1212**.

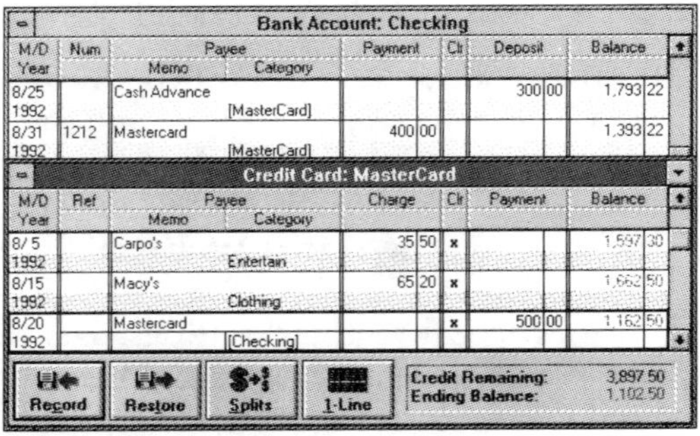

Figure 28.6 The transfer transaction that pays the MasterCard bill

5. Click on **Record** to save this transaction, and Quicken enters the other half of the transfer transaction into the Mastercard account. (The MasterCard register is also opened in Figure 28.6 so that you can see both sides of the transfer transaction.)

29

Mortgage and House Basis Accounts

Creating a Mortgage Account

If you want to keep track of a mortgage, you'll need to create an Other Liability account. (See Lesson 25.) For the purpose of this exercise, let's say that as of 8/1/92 you have a mortgage balance of $159,690.85. With the Other Liability account assigned the settings in Figure 29.1, you can then allocate mortgage payments to interest (an expense) and principal (repayment of a liability).

The Mortgage Register

The first time you open a liability register, such as the Mortgage register shown in Figure 29.2, you may be taken aback by the terminology Quicken uses for the fields. Don't be; they work much the same as the fields in a bank account, with one twist. Since a mortgage is a liability, a payment of principal belongs in the Decrease field, and decreases the outstanding balance.

Figure 29.1 Creating a mortgage
liability account

Any increase to the mortgage balance, such as deferred
interest, is entered in the Increase field, and increases
the outstanding balance.

Tip
Since individuals use a cash basis for tax purposes (rather than an accrual basis), create a
non-tax-related category to record deferred interest, which can't be expensed until paid.

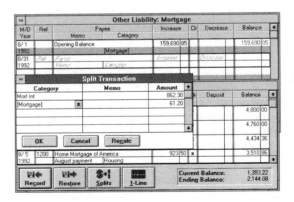

Figure 29.2 Allocating a mortgage payment
to principal and interest

Allocating a Mortgage Payment to Principal and Interest

Splitting a transaction and including a transfer transaction within the split enables you to allocate a mortgage payment to principal and interest. In Figure 29.2, for example, suppose you want to allocate check 1200—the $923.50 mortgage payment made on 8/5/92—to principal and interest. Let's assume that this is an adjustable rate mortgage and the next statement indicates that $862.30 went to interest and the remaining $61.20 to principal.

Tip

To create a loan amortization table, see Lesson 30.

Here's how to allocate this mortgage payment (or one of your own):

1. Open the Mortgage and Checking registers by clicking on to open the Account List window and then double-clicking on the **Mortgage account** and the **Checking account**. Then double-click on the **Account List window control box** to close this window. (It's not necessary to keep the Mortgage register open, but it will let you see what happens in each of the accounts.)

2. In the Checking register window, scroll to check 1200 on 8/5/92 and then click on its **Category** field.

3. Click on **Splits** at the bottom of the register to open the Split Transaction dialog box. Split the

923.50 transaction between principal and interest by first entering the amount of interest. In the first line, type **Mo** and Quicken fills in **Mort Int**. (Or open the Category & Transfer List window and choose from there.) Press **Tab twice** to move to the Amount field and type the amount of interest, **862.30**. When you press **Tab** to move to the second line, Quicken subtracts this amount from the 923.50 transaction amount and shows the difference of 61.20 on the next line.

4. Allocate the remaining amount, **61.20** in this case, to the Mortgage account as a transfer. In this example, type **[** and Quicken completes **[Checking]**, the first account listed in the Category List. Press **+** to cycle through the alphabetized account listings in the Category & Transfer List window or type **Mo** so that **[Mortgage]** appears. Your screen should now look like Figure 29.2.

5. Assign this split to the transaction by clicking on **OK**. Quicken returns you to the check 1200 transaction in the Checking register window, where --Splits-- appears in the Category field indicating that the transaction is split.

6. In the Checking register window, click on **Record** to save the split transaction.

7. Repeat Steps 2 through 6 and split the 9/1/92 check 1211 mortgage payment, $860.70 to mortgage interest and the remaining $62.80 to principal. You can see in Figure 29.3 how Quicken shows the corresponding transfer transaction in the Mortgage register reflecting the $61.20 payment of principal. The Ending Balance in the Mortgage checking register should be $159,566.85.

Other Liability: Mortgage							
M/D Year	Ref	Payee / Memo / Category	Increase	Clr	Decrease	Balance	
8/ 1 1992		Opening Balance / [Mortgage]	159,690 85			159,690 85	
8/ 5 1992		Home Mortgage of America / August payment [Checking]			61 20	159,629 65	
9/ 1 1992		Home Mortgage of America / [Checking]			62 80	159,566 85	

Bank Account: Checking							
M/D Year	Num	Payee / Memo / Category	Payment	Clr	Deposit	Balance	
9/ 1 1992	1210	Coast Savings and Loan / Auto:Loan	325 64			1,067 58	
9/ 1 1992	1211	Home Mortgage of America / --Splits--	923 50			144 08	
9/ 1 1992		Transfer to Checking / [Savings]			2,000 00	2,144 08	

Record	Restore	Splits	1-Line		Current Balance:	1,393.22
					Ending Balance:	2,144.08

Figure 29.3   The transaction after closing
the Open Splits dialog box

Tracking Your Home as an Asset

By keeping track of the flip side of a mortgage—the
asset value or *basis* of your home—you can use
Quicken to create net worth reports and maintain a
record of home improvements that you'll need should
you ever decide to sell.

To do this, create an Asset account called House (or, if
you move often, use the address instead) using the
amount you paid for the house as the beginning balance.
For instance, try creating the House account shown in
Figure 29.4 or one for your own home. (See Lesson 25).

Through the Splits Transaction dialog box, you can
create transfer transactions to allocate any changes in
the home value. For example, home improvements
would get allocated in Figure 29.5 as an Increase to the
Balance (basis). A Decrease to the basis rarely happens
until you sell the home.

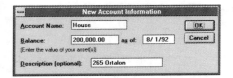

Figure 29.4   Creating an asset account
for a house

 Tip

Before you begin allocating that paint job, make
sure that you review the IRS publication about
home improvements. Many improvements,
such as painting, are considered maintenance
rather than an increase to the house basis if
performed more than 90 days before the sale of
the home.

M/D Year	Ref	Payee Memo Category	Decrease	Clr	Increase	Balance
8/1 1992		Opening Balance [House]			200,000 00	200,000 00
8/31 1992	*Ref*	*Payee* *Memo* *Category*	*Decrease*		*Increase*	

Other Asset: House

Record   Restore   Splits   1-Line   Ending Balance: 200,000.00

Figure 29.5   The house register window

30

Amortizing Loan Payments

What is a Loan Amortization Table?

Quicken provides an easy way you can create a *loan amortization* table allocating each loan payment, for a mortgage perhaps, to interest and principal. After you create this table, you can recall a particular payment as a memorized transaction.

Tip
Make sure you check out the Activities Financial Planners command, which you can use to create all sorts of loan amortization schedules and to perform what-if analyses.

Setting up the Amortization Table

Let's set up an amortization table for the $156,690.85 mortgage for which a Liability account was created in

Figure 30.1   Setting up an amortization table

Lesson 29. Here's how to do this (or to set up one for a loan of your own):

1. Open the Memorized Transaction List window by pressing **Ctrl+T**, the shortcut for the Lists Memorized Transaction command. Then click on **New** at the bottom of the window to open the Create Memorized Transaction dialog box shown in Figure 30.1.

2. Specify descriptive information about the memorized transaction. In this case, click on the **Payment** radio button. (If you're going to print a check from Quicken, accept Check.) Then click in the **Payee** text box and type **Home Mortgage of America**. Click in the **Amount** text box and type the monthly payment, **923.50**. (Don't worry if your mortgage is adjustable—you can later change the payment.) Don't enter Memo and Category information at this point. Instead, click on **Amortize** to open the dialog box shown in Figure 30.2.

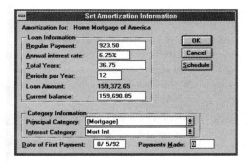

Figure 30.2 Specifying loan amortization information

3. Specify financial information for the loan. The first time you open the Set Amortization Information dialog box, you'll see the payment amount you just specified, 923.50 here, a 0% interest rate, and a 1 year term of 12 monthly payments. You'll need to enter:

- The **Annual Interest Rate** of the loan in decimal form, such as 6.25%.
- The **Total Years** remaining on the loan in decimal form, such as 36.75 for 36 years and 9 months.
- The **Periods per Year**, or the number of payments per year, usually 12.
- The **Current Balance** of the loan, 159,690.85 in this example. Notice that the **Loan Amount** of 159,372.65, which Quicken calculates from the other values, differs slightly from the actual current balance.

⇨ **Note:** If your bank computes interest daily or based on the actual days in a month, the amortization Quicken creates may differ from that which the bank calculates.

4. Assign principal to the Mortgage account by clicking in the **Principal Category** text box and then typing **[Mortgage]** or clicking on ▣ and choosing from the drop-down list that appears. (If you haven't created such an account, see Lesson 29.) Likewise, click in the **Interest Category** text box, and then type **Mort Int** to assign interest to this category.

5. Click in the **Date of First Payment** text box, and type the date of the next payment date, **8/5/92** in this case. Then accept the Payments Made setting of **0**.

6. Click on **Schedule** to view the amortization table of this mortgage shown in Figure 30.3. (To print a copy of this schedule, click on Print.)

7. Click on **OK twice** to close the amortization table and create the memorized transaction shown in Figure 30.4.

From the Memorized Transaction List window, you can edit or delete an amortized loan payment just like any other memorized transaction. See Lesson 19.

Assigning a Memorized Loan Amortization Transaction

Once you've created an amortized memorized transaction like the one in Figure 30.4, you recall it just like any other memorized transaction. That is, you begin

Date	Pmt	Principal	Interest	Balance	
			6.25%	159,690.85	
8/ 5/92	1	91.78	831.72	159,599.07	
9/ 5/92	2	92.25	831.25	159,506.82	
10/ 5/92	3	92.74	830.76	159,414.08	
11/ 5/92	4	93.22	830.28	159,320.86	
12/ 5/92	5	93.70	829.80	159,227.16	
1/ 5/93	6	94.19	829.31	159,132.97	
2/ 5/93	7	94.68	828.82	159,038.29	
3/ 5/93	8	95.18	828.32	158,943.11	
4/ 5/93	9	95.67	827.83	158,847.44	
5/ 5/93	10	96.17	827.33	158,751.27	

Figure 30.3 The amortization table

typing in the Payee field of a new transaction until Quicken recalls it, or you can choose it from the Payee drop-down list or the Memorized Transaction List window. (See Lesson 19.)

When Quicken recalls the memorized amortized loan payment, you'll see the dialog box in Figure 30.5 giving you a chance to change any of the settings for the particular payment you are making. For example, you can change the interest rate for a loan that changes monthly or add a prepayment of principal. When you click on OK, Quicken enters the transaction in the register.

⇨ **Note:** Any changes you make here will affect the loan amortization schedule.

Description	Amount	Type	Spl	Memo	Category	Clr	Grp
Coast Savings and Loan	325.64	Pmt		August pay...		1	
Computer Currents	159.00	Pmt			Subscriptions		
Deposit	250.00	Dep		Bond Int 6/30			
Home Mortgage of Am.	923.50	Pmt	A		Mortgage		
Home Mortgage of Am.	923.50	Pmt		August pay...		1	
Internal Revenue Serv...	1,560.60	Chk		Estimated t...	TaxFed		
Larry Yen	240.50	Pmt		Dentist for ...	Medical		

Figure 30.4 The memorized loan amortization

Figure 30.5　Adjusting a specific payment

Undoing an Amortized Loan Payment

Whenever you recall a memorized amortized loan payment, Quicken gets ready for the next time by increasing the Payments Made setting by one in Set Amortization Information dialog box shown in Figure 30.2. If you mistakenly recall this transaction an extra time in the register, you need to

- Delete the transaction in the register.
- Use the Memorized Transaction List window and the Edit button to edit the transaction and adjust the Payments Made setting down by 1 in the Set Amortization Information dialog box.

♦ *Lesson* ♦

31

Reports and Graphs

Quicken Report Types

Quicken provides a number of reports—all accessible through the Reports Home command—you can use for taxes and to summarize your financial status. Table 31.1 lists these reports and what each one contains. As just one example, Figure 31.1 shows a Tax Summary report created for the transactions demonstrated in this book.

The quality of many reports—especially the Tax Summary and Tax Schedule reports—depend on how you've set up your Category list for tax purposes, whether you've assigned Federal forms to categories, and how faithfully you've assigned transactions to categories. If you're not familiar with how this works, review Lesson 22.

Each of these report types is generated, viewed, and printed in the same way. And, as you become comfort-

Table 31.1 Standard Quicken Reports

Report	Produces
Cash Flow	Net cash flow statement: cash inflows (income categories) less cash outflows (expense categories). (See Figure 31.3.)
Net Worth	Net worth statement (assets less liabilities). Assets and liabilities totalled by account type.
Monthly Budget	Compares actual category amounts, by month, to budgeted category amounts.
Itemized Categories	Transaction detail and balances for all categories and subcategories.
Tax Summary	Transaction detail and balances for tax-related categories.
Tax Schedule	Transaction detail and balances for categories assigned to a Federal tax form. (See Figure 31.1.)

able with Quicken and explore its custom report generating capability, you'll find that these reports share many of the same options.

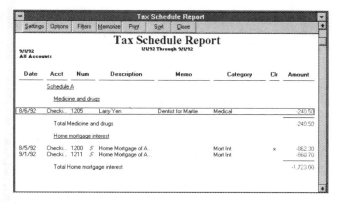

Figure 31.1 A Tax Summary report

Generating a Report

Let's generate a cash flow report for the financial data entered throughout this book. To do this or to generate a report for your own data:

1. Select the **Reports Home** command and then the report type, **Cash Flow** in this case. You'll see the window shown in Figure 31.2.

➡ **Note:** You'll see virtually the same dialog box shown in Figure 31.2 for all the Home report types. The exception is the Net Worth Report, which generates a report containing balances on a specific date.

2. If you want, type a report name of up to 39 characters in the Report Title text box. If you don't include a title, Quicken uses the report

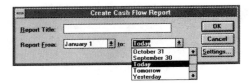

Figure 31.2 Generating a report

name shown in the title bar. For instance, if we don't enter a title here, Quicken will use "Cash Flow Report."

3. Specify the months that the report should cover. Quicken automatically enters the first month of the current year in the first date text box, January 1 here, and Today in the second. Accept these settings, although you can click on ▼ and choose another option from the drop-down list shown.

4. Click on **OK** to generate the report. Figure 31.3 shows the cash flow report Quicken generates.

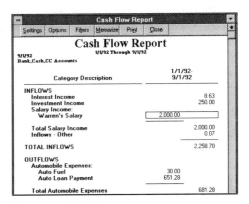

Figure 31.3 A cash flow report

Viewing a Report

The window a report appears in, such as the cash flow report (just generated), may be used to scroll through and view information. In addition, from there you can switch to a register window, make changes, and immediately view the results in the report.

A report window also has QuickZoom features you might want to take advantage of. For example, the cursor changes to ℚ whenever it nears a category or subcategory total. Double-click, and Quicken opens a zoom window offering a magnified view of the area. Double-click on the window control box ▣ to close the Zoom window or a report window.

Printing a Report

Once you generate a report, such as the Cash Flow report in Figure 31.3, it's a simple matter to print it. With the report window open:

1. In the report window, click on the ▭ button. This accesses the same dialog box shown in Figure 31.4 just as if you had used the File Report Printer command.
2. Accept the Print to option, **Printer**, to output to your printer in high-quality graphics mode.

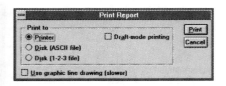

Figure 31.4 Printing a report

3. If you're using a dot-matrix printer that includes a compressed font, click on the **Draft-mode printing** check box to print the register in this font.

If you're using a laserjet printer that doesn't include a compressed font, turning on Draft-mode printing will result in blank pages being output.

4. If your printer is capable of graphics—a laserjet or inkjet—click on the **Use graphic line drawing** check box to tell Quicken to use graphic line characters when printing. (This option has no effect if you're using a dot-matrix printer.) When you don't check this option, Quicken single-underlines all subtotals using underscores and double-underlines all grand totals using equal (=) signs.
5. Click on **Print** to begin printing. While Quicken is printing, you'll see a message indicating where the report is printing. Click on **Cancel** at any time to cancel printing.

Creating Graphs

A graph can visually present your financial data in a way that no report can. For example, here's how to create a graph of the Cash Flow report data in Figure 31.3:

1. Click on in the IconBar, the shortcut for the Reports Graphs command. You'll see the Create

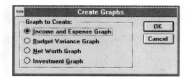

Figure 31.5 Choosing the graph type

Graphs dialog box shown in Figure 31.5 listing the available graph types.

2. Accept the default, **Income and Expense Graph**, by clicking on **OK**. You'll now see the dialog box in Figure 31.6. Although you can use some of the options to limit graphed data, the most important option is the time frame. Since data has only been entered since 8/1/92, type **8/92** in the first text box. (Usually it's best to graph no more than one year of data.)

3. Click on **Graph**, and you'll see the graph shown in Figure 31.7.

▷ **Note:** The Graph Preferences command provides options that change the appearance of a graph.

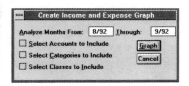

Figure 31.6 Specifying the time frame

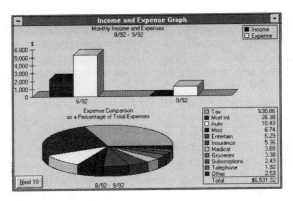

Figure 31.7   An income and expense graph

Working in a Graph Window

Quicken's QuickZoom provides some handy features you should keep in mind when working with graphs. For example, suppose the cursor is positioned over the second (right) 8/92 bar in Figure 31.7 so that it appears as ⌕ :

- Left-click to see the value this bar represents.
- Double-click to see a pie chart for the 8/92 data only. Within this second graph, double-clicking on any slice opens a report window showing the categories the slice represents.
- Pressing SHIFT while clicking hides both of the 8/92 bars, although this data is still included in the pie graph. (To restore the graph, you must recreate it.)

Printing a Graph

To print a graph that is currently open, simply click on in the IconBar or press Ctrl+P, the shortcut for the File Print Graph command. Keep in mind that Quicken uses the settings currently assigned through the File Print Setup Report/Graph Printer Setup command. (See Lesson 32.) If your printer supports color, choose the Preferences Graphs command and turn on Print in Color.

♦ *Lesson* ♦

32

Customizing Printer Settings for Reports

Selecting the Report Printer

When you print reports, Quicken outputs to the default Windows printer. If you want to customize a report by changing printer settings, you must first select the report printer. For example, here's how to select an HP LaserJet III or another printer:

1. Choose the **File Printer Setup** command. Then choose **Report/Graph Printer Setup**. Figure 32.1 shows the dialog box that you'll see.
2. Click on ▣ to open the **Printer** drop-down list where the available printers are listed alphabetically. If you haven't previously changed the report printer, the first printer in this list is chosen.

➡ **Note:** The entries you see in the Printer drop-down list no doubt differ from those you see in Figure 32.1, depending on the Windows printer drivers you've installed.

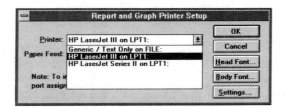

Figure 32.1 The Report and Graph Printer
Setup dialog box

3. Choose the printer. In this case, click on **HP
LaserJet III on LPT1:**. Then click on **OK** to
confirm this settings.

Printing in Landscape

When printing a report, Quicken adjusts the width of
the fields in the printed output so that the entire report
fits on 8.5 x 11 inch paper. As a result, certain fields—
for example, memo fields and category fields—may be
truncated (cut off). You can usually solve this problem
by changing the printer orientation to landscape (sideways). Landscape printing allows for longer lines per
page but fewer of them.

If, for example, you're currently printing on a
LaserJet III printer connected to LPT1, follow these
steps to change this printer (or any other printer) to
landscape mode:

1. Choose the **File Printer Setup Re-
port/Graph Printer Setup** command to access the dialog box shown in Figure 32.1. If the
Printer setting isn't **HP LaserJet III on LPT1:**,

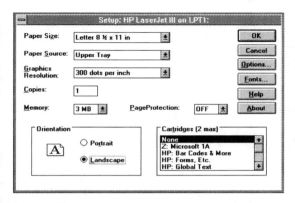

Figure 32.2 The HP LaserJet III printer driver
dialog box

you need to change it. (See "Selecting the Report
Printer," above.)

2. Click on **Settings** to see the printer driver dialog
box for the currently selected printer. For example, Figure 32.2 shows the dialog box for the HP
LaserJet III printer. (The one you see for your
printer may differ.)

 The dialog box you see here is the same one you
see when you use the Windows Control Panel
to set up your printer. In fact, what you're doing
here is changing the printer setup for Windows,
and therefore, for all Windows applications.
Therefore, when you've completed this exercise,
remember to change the Orientation setting
back to portrait, otherwise, all your Windows
print jobs will be printed in landscape.

3. To change the Orientation setting to Landscape, click on the **Landscape** radio button.

4. Click on **OK** to confirm these settings. Now, when you print your report, Quicken will print it in landscape.

Changing Fonts

By default, all headings in a report are printed in 12-point Courier; all other text is printed in 10-point Courier. If you like, you can change the typefaces and the point sizes that Quicken uses to print your reports. Note that changing the point size will enable you to fit more or less text in the same space. (Points are a measure of the height of a character; a *point* is about 1/72 of an inch.)

Try this approach to change the font of all text, except headings to 8-point Courier. The steps are the same to pick any other typeface and point size:

1. Select the **File Printer Setup Report/Graph Printer Setup** command to access the dialog box in Figure 32.1. The Head Font governs the typeface of report headings; the Body Font controls the font of all other printed text. In this case, click on **Body Font** and you'll see the dialog box in Figure 32.3.

2. Change the typeface by scrolling through the **Font** list and clicking on **Arial**. (Depending on the typeface chosen, you may also be abe to assign an attribute such as italics or bold in the Font Style list.)

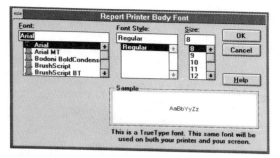

Figure 32.3 The Report Printer Body Font dialog box

⇨ **Note:** The available fonts in the list are determined by Windows, the currently selected report
printer, and any third-party font packages that
you've installed in Windows, such as Bitstream's
Facelift or the Adobe Type Manager (ATM).

3. Change the point size by scrolling through the
Size list and clicking on **8**. (Available point sizes
will vary, depending on the typeface. If you've
chosen a TrueType font, you can enter any point
size even if it's not included in the list.)

4. Click on **OK** to confirm these settings. Quicken
will use 8-point Arial for all text except the headings, which will be printed using the 12-point
Courier settings left unchanged.

◆ *Lesson* ◆

33

Using Quicken for a Business

Businesses That Can Use Quicken?

Virtually any type of business can use Quicken for Windows as its accounting package; however, it works better for some than others. Quicken is designed for a business, especially a sole proprietorship, without too many transactions of any one type, and for which most transactions flow through (occur in) a bank account, such as checking. Therefore, a business that must track 2,000 clients individually may find another accounting package much more efficient than Quicken. Quicken, however, may still be the right accounting package for all other financial transactions of the company.

If your company is an S or C corporation (these are IRS delineations), you can use Quicken as your financial accounting package with a little jerryrigging of the stockholder accounts. (See "Setting up Stockholder Accounts" later in this lesson.)

One final comment about Quicken as a business financial system: It's a great place to begin, even if your company will need a more traditional or custom financial package down the road. When you do switch over, just export or enter the Quicken account balances into the new system.

 Note: For a business using cash-based accounting, only cleared transactions up to a specific date, such as 12/31, count. For an accrual-based business, all transactions up to a specific date, like 12/31, count.

How Quicken Handles Double-Entry Bookkeeping

If you're at all familiar with the traditional double-entry bookkeeping system, you'll know that every transaction is entered as a debit and credit in a general ledger. Below is a typical entry you would make in a general ledger:

	Debit	**Credit**
Phone Expense	125	
Cash:Checking		125

In a general ledger system, each side of the transaction is posted to the respective account, as in this example in which a 125 debit is recorded in the phone expense account and 125 credit is recorded in the checking account.

In Quicken, you don't need a general ledger to create these entries. Quicken streamlines the process by making one important assumption about a business: *the majority of transactions flow through bank accounts*, such as checking. This allows you to enter a transaction such as phone expense once in a bank account register. In essence, you're entering one side of a two-sided entry.

The Category & Transfer List is the key to creating the second side of the entry. Remember, you use the Category & Transfer List to assign income and expense categories, as well as to create transfer transactions between accounts. This means that every time you assign a category or an account from the Category & Transfer List, you are actually creating the other side of the double entry. Assign the cash transaction paying the phone bill to the Telephone category, for instance, and you've created (posted) the other half of the two-sided entry. In Quicken, you're performing double-entry bookkeeping in a much easier, yet logical manner.

It's especially important when using Quicken for a business that every transaction contain a category or transfer account in the Category field; otherwise, the second side of an entry doesn't occur and your balance sheet won't balance.

Setting Up Business Accounts and Categories

Setting up Quicken for a business really isn't any different than doing so for home use. The accounts (especially the number of accounts) and categories you use will differ, however. For example, you'll probably want to set up quite a few Other Asset and Other Liability accounts. Use Other Asset accounts for receivables, equipment, deposits, prepaid expenses, and so on. Create Other Liability accounts for trade payables, federal and state taxes (employee and employer) payable, loans, and credit lines.

If you want to track customers or clients individually, you can set up specific accounts and categories for them. For example, an important customer would be represented by a A/R (accounts receivable) asset account and an income subcategory. Another alternative would be to create a separate class for each customer.

You'll also want to customize the Category & Transfer List to reflect the expenses and sources of income for your particular business. If you need to, reinstall Quicken and specify business, or home and business use.

Creating Stockholder Equity Accounts

If your business is a C corporation, you'll need to set up stockholder equity and retained earnings accounts. In Quicken, these are simply Other Liability accounts that you name Stockholder Equity and Retained Earnings. If your business is a partnership, use the same approach except create multiple equity accounts, one for each partner.

Tying Income and Retained Earnings Together

One of the limitations of Quicken as a business accounting package is that it doesn't automatically create a relationship between income and retained earnings. Instead, if your business is a C corporation, you have to create the relationship through transactions.

Consider, for a moment, how a typical accounting package works. When you close a period, such as a month, quarter, or year, an accounting package automatically adds the income (or loss) from that period to retained earnings. When you generate a balance sheet, the income is included in retained earnings, and everything balances (at least in theory).

Quicken, on the other hand, never creates such a transaction, even when you close the year. Therefore, whenever you want to create a balance sheet, you must first generate an income statement and then create a transaction in the Retained Earnings account equal to this income. (This is the one transaction that must *not* be assigned a category.) Otherwise, your balance sheet will *never* balance.

Tip

If the balance sheet doesn't balance after you add the income transaction, look for some transactions without entries in the Category field.

Information to Generate Outside of Quicken

Although Quicken's system of accounts and categories works well to record transactions, there's no good way to provide detail about many transactions that you compute from other values. What's more, the register approach doesn't always display information as you'd expect to see it.

For example, an equipment schedule is usually created as a listing of each asset and its corresponding deprecation across a row. By summing down columns (years), you can calculate the depreciation expense for a given year. Rather than struggling with Quicken to create a custom report that poses as an asset and depreciation schedule, many times it's easier to generate this detail information outside of Quicken. (In fact, by creating such a schedule in a spreadsheet program like Excel, the schedule will automatically be updated should any underlying numbers change, such as the depreciation rate.) In Quicken, you would then enter transactions reflecting depreciation expense and accumulated depreciation in total.

34

Year-End Operations

Year-End Operations

Here are some things that you should do at year-end to maintain a sound financial system:

- Print year-end reports. Lesson 31 describes how to do this.
- Decide whether to archive files or start a new year. Read the following sections before deciding which you prefer.
- Create back-up copies of these files.

Tip

Before you archive your files or start a new year, make sure that you have received your January statements and reconciled your accounts.

Archiving Data Files

The term *archiving* has a unique definition in Quicken. It means making a new copy of the current file but

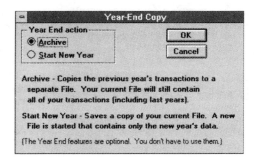

Figure 34.1 The Year-End dialog box

including in the copy only those transactions dated earlier than the current year. For example, if you archive the current file at any point in 1993, Quicken creates a file containing all transactions up to and including December 31, 1992. This means, for example, that if you've been working in Quicken since 1990, the archive file will contain all the transactions from 1990, 1991, and 1992.

The benefit to archiving is that each archived file contains all transactions entered in Quicken up to the end of that year. If one of the archive files becomes corrupted, the most data you ever lose is one year's worth. Even then, you can use the current QDATA files to recreate an archive file for that year.

To archive a file in Quicken:

1. Select the **File Year-End Copy** command to access the dialog box shown in Figure 34.1.
2. Click on the **Archive** radio button and then click on **OK**. You'll now see the dialog box shown in Figure 34.2.

Figure 34.2 Archiving the current file

3. Specify the name of the archive copy. Since the default file name is QDATA and the current year is 1993, Quicken suggests the name QDATA92 for the archive file. Although we'll accept this name, you can enter any eight-character name you like.

4. Specify the dates of the transactions to be included in the archive copy. Quicken suggests all the transactions prior to and including 12/31/92. Accept this setting and create the archive file by clicking on OK.

Quicken creates a file called QDATA92 in C:\QUICKENW containing all transactions up to and including December 31, 1992. The QDATA file you work with every time you open Quicken is not affected.

Starting a New Year

Like archiving, *starting a new year* has a special meaning in Quicken. When you start a new year, Quicken creates a copy of the current file and saves it under a different name. It then *shrinks* the current file to contain only these elements:

- Ending account balances, which become the beginning account balances for the new year
- Any transactions dated in the new year
- All investment transactions
- All uncleared transactions

The first benefit to starting a new year this way is that your QDATA file isn't cluttered with old information. Second, the disk space required to store the files for the prior year is much smaller than archiving because each file contains only the details (transactions) for that year. The trade-off is that if one of these files gets corrupted or erased, then you've lost the data for that year. Make sure that you keep additional backup copies on floppies just in case disaster strikes.

Tip

If you don't do your taxes until the last possible minute, you may not want to shrink your file until then.

To demonstrate how to start a new year, let's assume that the current file is QDATA, and that it contains transactions from 1991 and 1992. In addition, the current date is 3/1/93. Here are the steps:

1. Select the **File Year-End Copy** command to access the dialog box shown in Figure 34.1.

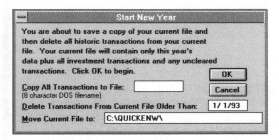

Figure 34.3 Starting a new year

2. Click on the **Start New Year** radio button and then click on **OK** to confirm. You'll now see the dialog box shown in Figure 34.3.
3. In the first text box, type a name for the copy Quicken will make of the current QDATA files for 1992. For instance, type a descriptive name up to eight characters, like **QDATA_92**.
4. Specify what Quicken should do with the QDATA file for the upcoming year, 1993 in this case. Accept the date **1/1/93** in the second text box, which tells Quicken to delete all transactions before 1/1/93 in the QDATA file. Likewise, accept **C:\QUICKENW** in the third text box, which says to keep the QDATA files for the new year in this directory.
5. Click on **OK** to confirm these settings.

First, Quicken copies QDATA to QDATA_92, which contains all of the transaction detail for 1992. It then updates QDATA by making the 1992 ending balances the 1993 beginning balances and deletes all transactions before 1/1/93 except investment and uncleared transactions.

Backing Up Files

Backing up your files is a way to protect yourself should your hard disk fail or you inadvertently delete some important data. The steps to back up the current QDATA files to drive B are given below. Use the same procedure to create a backup for a year-end copy:

1. Select the **File Backup** command to access the dialog box shown in Figure 34.4.
2. To back up the current QDATA files, click on the **Current File** radio button. (To backup other files, click on the **Select From List** radio button. Later, when you click on OK, Quicken will display a dialog box allowing you to select a file.)
3. Specify the drive in which you want Quicken to place the backup copy. To specify drive B:, click on ⬛ to open the Backup Drive drop-down list. Then click on B:.
4. Click on **OK** to begin the backup process. When Quicken is done, you'll see a message telling you this. Click on **OK** again.

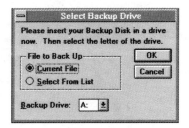

Figure 34.4 Backing up a file

Epilogue
Where to Go from Here

Although this book gives you a good basic understanding of Quicken for Windows, there are several intermediate and advanced topics that it does not discuss. This list briefly describes some that you may want to investigate:

- **Investment accounts**—Quicken is adept at helping you keep track of your stocks, bonds, mutual funds, and other investments. In fact, you may have noticed many grayed commands as you explored Quicken's menus; many of these relate to investment accounts. Before working with investment accounts, though, become proficient with the material described in this book.

- **Paying bills electronically**—If you have a modem, you can pay your bills electronically using Quicken. To do so, you must first sign up with CheckFree, a separate electronic bill-paying service. You can then set up Quicken to use your modem and transmit information to CheckFree.

- **Budgeting**—Quicken also has features for budgeting (although we've found them somewhat inflexible and hard to set up).
- **Custom reports**—Quicken has a variety of custom report features. Once you begin to explore them, you'll realize that you can create almost any kind of report.
- **Importing and exporting files**—You can import and export ASCII files using Quicken's File commands. You can also create DDE (Dynamic Data Exchange) links between Quicken and Microsoft Excel to share data between these applications.
- **Exporting data to a tax package**—When it comes time to do your taxes, you can export your Quicken data to a special tax package, like TurboTax.

Index